CW00459406

Set design by Alexander Dodge   Costume design by Anita Yavich   Photo by Michal Daniel

A scene from the The Public Theater production of *Measure for Pleasure* in New York City.

MEASURE FOR PLEASURE

A RESTORATION ROMP
BY DAVID GRIMM

★

★

DRAMATISTS
PLAY SERVICE
INC.

MEASURE FOR PLEASURE
Copyright © 2006, David Grimm

All Rights Reserved

SPECIAL NOTE

Developed with the assistance of the Sundance Institute.

Originally Produced at
The Public Theater in March 2006;
Mara Manus, Executive Director; Oskar Eustis, Artistic Director.

To Paul and Paul and Paul

ACKNOWLEDGMENTS

My deepest thanks to Patrick Herold, Morgan Jenness, George C. Wolfe, Oskar Eustis, Jocelyn Clarke, Celise Kalke, Michael Kenyon, Maria Goyanes, David Benedict, Eleanor Holdridge, and all the wonderful writers at New Dramatists. Special thanks to Philip Himberg and the Sundance Theatre Lab (and the casting genius of Meg Simon and John Power); also to Kate Pakenham and Ari Edelson of the Old Vic New Voices Program in London (and the marvelous cast of actors and director Angus Jackson); and to Gaye Smith and Primary Stages. The journey of this play could not have taken place, however, without the talent, insight, and patience of two very dear men: Michael Stuhlbarg, for whom I wrote the role of Blunt and who is without a doubt one of our national theatrical treasures; and Peter Dubois, an incredible director, an amazing friend and a fellow member of Club Condor.

—*David Grimm*

MEASURE FOR PLEASURE was originally produced by The Public Theater in New York City, opening on February 21, 2006. It was directed by Peter DuBois; the set design was by Alexander Dodge; the costume design was by Anita Yavich; the lighting design was by Christopher Akerlind; the original music was by Peter Golub; the sound design was by Walter Trarbach and Tony Smolenski IV; the style consultant was B.H. Barry; the production stage manager was Jane Pole; and the assistant stage manager was Elizabeth Miller. The cast was as follows:

WILL BLUNT .... Michael Stuhlbarg
SIR PETER LUSTFORTH .... Wayne Knight
CAPTAIN DICK DASHWOOD .... Saxon Palmer
MOLLY TAWDRY .... Euan Morton
LADY VANITY LUSTFORTH .... Suzanne Bertish
DAME STICKLE .... Susan Blommaert
HERMIONE GOODE .... Emily Swallow
FOOTMEN .... Frederick Hamilton, Ryan Tresser

CHARACTERS
(in order of appearance)

WILL BLUNT — valet to Sir Peter Lustforth. Roughly 28. Curious, troublesome, quixotic; a prankster, though never malicious; a romantic afraid of his nature.

SIR PETER LUSTFORTH — a landed country gentleman of about 60. Though of lower birth and a rough frame, he has risen in the ranks through cleverness and subterfuge.

CAPTAIN DICK DASHWOOD — a handsome rake of about 30; an epicure, seducer, and sensualist, given to wine, women, and grandiosity.

MOLLY TAWDRY — a 20-year-old male prostitute passing himself as a woman. Though experience has hardened him, there is still much of the boy about him.

LADY VANITY LUSTFORTH — wife to Sir Peter Lustforth. In her mid-50s. A woman of great elegance and grace who hides her heart beneath a conceit of excessive pride.

DAME STICKLE — a puritan lady in her 50s. Practical and meddlesome; her fierce belief in a proper Christian way of life dictates her views and actions.

HERMIONE GOODE — a beautiful country lass of 25; niece of Dame Stickle. Though her appearance might make her seem flighty, she has a keen wit, a quick mind, and a passionate nature.

SETTING

In the City and in the Country, 1751, during the forty days known in the Christian Calendar as Lent, which end with the Spring Solstice.

"Do not be afraid of the past. If people tell you that it is irrevocable, do not believe them. The past, the present and the future are but one moment in the sight of God, in whose sight we should try to live. Time and space, succession and extension, are merely accidental conditions of thought. The imagination can transcend them."

—*Oscar Wilde*

MEASURE FOR PLEASURE

Prologue

Blunt enters from the audience.

BLUNT.
Ladies and gentlemen, before we start this play —
Yes, kindly lend your ears, I have a couple things to say.
The management requests — Hey you, don't scoff! —
That you oblige us here and turn your cell phones off.
If you've got cough drops, candy, gum, be kind, unwrap them
  now.
If that's too difficult for you, an usher there will show you how.
Come on. Let's have it. Now! Not once the play begins.
(A beat.) Seriously. I mean it.
And if some tit comes late, feel free to kick him in the shins.
I mean, how hard is it to get here and make sure that you're
  on time?
It's not like you were asked to come and stand on stage and rhyme!
(A beat.) Thank you, madam.
And no recording implements or cameras, you got that?
  Right. Enough from me.
Oh yes, there's one more thing: I hope you've all had a nice pee;
'Cos nothing do I hate more than that noxious egotist
Who, restless, comes and goes and whispers, "Tell me what I
  missed!"
So settle in, get comfortable, but please don't fall asleep.
(A beat.) Yes, sir, I'm talking to you.
Remember that you paid for this, and theatre ain't cheap.
All right, let's have the houselights out so we can start the show.
The sooner we get underway, the sooner you can go. *(He exits.)*

ACT ONE

Scene 1

The Lustforth home. Clothing, boots, and wig are strewn across the floor. Enter Sir Peter, wearing only a shirt. He dresses as he speaks.

LUSTFORTH *(Aside.)*
A worse affliction for a husband than a mistress who resists
Is having to come home to find a wife who still persists!
Not a quarter hour through the door, my boots and wig scarce off, but my good lady (damn the day I made her mine!) accosts me with coquettish ways, the like of which a woman half her age would blush to own. "Stallion," she calls me. Also "Hercules." And pouts her withered lip and bends as if to pick up a dropped fan, imagining in her dried addled brain her figure could inflame some passion. S'death! E'en twenty years ago before old age's hammer swung and shivered up her face like a cracked wall, she had no beauty worth remarking on. I rage, I cry, I reason, pointing out the only thing her body can bring up in me is half-digested lunch; yet she insists and I, like some enslaved somnambulist, oblige and — *(A groan of release and disgust.)* ! Meantime, the true and potent object of my lust, a virgin blossom fairly itching to be plucked, resists my every imprecation! Ah, but young Hermione is everything my wife is not — Where one is foul, the other is so fair; where one stinks up the house, the other does perfume the air. And oh, to see her, gentlemen, is to relive the call of youth! Egad, I'd give my arse to break her open like a ripened peach and lap up all the juices of her sighs! I am a man accursed, my friends. And such is my sad fate: To live in hope of her as I ride homeward, nursing my blue wrinkled balls, there to be greeted by a woman who resembles 'em! Ah good sirs, would that among you was a man both bold and brave enough who'd dare play substitute and ravish my foul gorgon of a wife, I could with haste attain betwixt my loins my beauty's golden fleece.

10

Yet this same man, if any God could curse him to existence, must be stalwart yet degenerate, undaunted yet depraved; in short — A lecher without standards for whom any hole will do. But know I such a sordid man? Do you? *(Blunt enters carrying a feather duster.)*

BLUNT. Sir, there's a man without.

LUSTFORTH. Without resources, then 'tis I! Without munitions or the strength to countermand her blasts. Tell Her Ladyship my feedbag's empty, boy. Tell her I'm dead, or fled to the Bahamas.

BLUNT. *(Aside.)* This is what I have to deal with seven days a week. *(Aloud.)* No, sir. There is a man outside what waits upon your pleasure.

LUSTFORTH. Pleasure? There's a word and meaning I have long forgot. What is this man?

BLUNT. He claims to be — No no, don't tell me; it'll come. *(Pause. Aside:)* Shit. Can I — Lemme see your program a minute, darling. *(Ad lib as he checks a program.)* Oh yes, that's it. *(Aloud.)* Captain Dick Dashwood, sir.

LUSTFORTH. Dash your impudence, you goose. Dick Dashwood's dead. I had report of his demise this fortnight last.

DASHWOOD. *(Entering.)* A sad report which may yet bear some truth if I'm to wait out in the hall much longer.

LUSTFORTH. Dick! Alive!

DASHWOOD. And thirsty. You there — Bring a bottle of your master's wine; and see it's not the rancid piss he serves his neighbors, or I'll clout you.

BLUNT. *(Exiting.)* Seeing as what little clout one has working this house, that is a kindly offer, sir. Hoo ha.

DASHWOOD. That servant wants a whipping.

LUSTFORTH. Dashwood, here you stand as hale and hardy as the day I last encountered you, when half the town has been at mourning over you these weeks — !

DASHWOOD. I'll wager t'other half of town has been a-celebrating on my death and all of them are husbands; those that mourn: their wives. Sir Peter, you must promise never to reveal the face behind the mask of my extinction.

LUSTFORTH. But of course, as a fellow member of our secret Order of the Knights of West Wycombe, you've my word on it.

DASHWOOD. Nay, list — Not even to our brother knights. A bond is made but to be broken, and those wags and lechers of our company love nothing more than scandal.

LUSTFORTH. You were most sorely missed at our last gathering.

11

'Oons but Dick, we had a strumpet there with tits like melons in high season. You should have seen as ten of us took turns at — Anyway, you have my word. The rest, as one dead poet has it, will be silence. *(Lustforth presents the secret greeting of the Order: each hand presenting horns with thumbs extended, held to his temples. He speaks the secret words:)* "In Venus' loins, by Hell's anointed — " *(Dashwood follows suit and joins in:)*

DASHWOOD and LUSTFORTH. " — Keep we our spirits true."

DASHWOOD. I knew if any man is to be trusted, then 'tis you. Sir Peter, I have reformed myself. *(Blunt reenters, holding a tray and swigging from a bottle of wine.)*

LUSTFORTH. What the christing devil — ?

BLUNT. *(Presenting it to Dashwood.)* Not bad for a Merlot. A bit fruity perhaps, but — *(Dashwood takes the bottle and cuffs Blunt in the head.)* Would you prefer the Cabernet? *(Lustforth cuffs Blunt in the head.)*

LUSTFORTH. You push me, Blunt.

BLUNT. I would, but where's a steep cliff when you need it? *(Lustforth raises his hand to strike again, but Blunt exits.)*

LUSTFORTH. You mustn't mind my fool; my anger pleases him. But Dashwood come, uncork thyself. Pour forth the vintage of your tale. My ears do thirst to taste its curious draught.

DASHWOOD. My story is a bitter grape, yet I will crush it thus: It doth involve a woman.

LUSTFORTH. Aye, as all good vintners can attest: 'Tis woman drives a man to wine.

DASHWOOD. 'Tis no mere whining this, Sir Peter, for I am in love.

LUSTFORTH. In love? Again? Pish, Dashwood, but you've drained the contents of that bottle many times. How can there be a drop left in't?

DASHWOOD. So did I think myself; yet by my troth, she fills me up anew.

LUSTFORTH. And so you long to fill her up.

DASHWOOD. No, friend, this love is true! No more for me th'inconstant life of a buzzing bee which passeth every changing hour by supping from a diff'rent flower. Her blossom yields all dreams and hopes.

LUSTFORTH. Then Dashwood, wherefore play the corpse? A lady hath no usage for a man who's dead, lest she be married to him.

DASHWOOD. Ah, if it were not for my ill-fame of having loved too often and too well, I would have had her even now. Yet that dear creature holds my heart to ransom for my past and will not give, even for begging, that which I have had most freely up 'til now.

LUSTFORTH. Ah women are such prudes! What boots it that a man must bed a sea of wenches, whores, and slatterns? Is't your fault you had to wade knee-deep in cunt before you found her? Man must do what man must do to find the island of his bliss.

DASHWOOD. And now I have! Rich promises I gave her, and cajolements — Oaths that I had changed my ways — But she would none of it. And so, to teach her not to take Dick Dashwood's yearning love for granted, I thought it best to kill him off. Rumors through gossip-mills had me quite dead within the week. The word began as pox, but somehow metamorphosized to losing at a duel — I've died a dozen deaths, my friend, yet in each one, her name was the last word to cross my lips. 'T'was handsomely portrayed, I'm told.

LUSTFORTH. But if Dick Dashwood's dead, how will he win her?

DASHWOOD. By new-minting! I will adopt some wily and ingenious guise and woo my love anew. I'll say I've come to town to seek my fortune. Or to see St Paul's and pray. Nay; a man of God would only be suspected for a lecher. Tosh, I'll fadge it well anon. What's most important is I act with haste, for I've a rival to her warm affections.

LUSTFORTH. What? A rival? How?

DASHWOOD. Alas, I've never seen the man. But I have heard he's three score old and of a face and form repellent. Egad, Sir Peter, but I'd shoot him dead if e'er he touched my sweet and pure Hermione.

LUSTFORTH. *(Aside.)* Hermione? Nay, could it be — ? *(Aloud.)* What sort of woman is this — this — ?

DASHWOOD. Hermione Goode. She is niece and ward to one Dame Stickle, a puritan residing hard by Bishopsgate.

LUSTFORTH. *(Aside.)* By hell's own breath, what fickle fate!

DASHWOOD. You say — ?

LUSTFORTH. She is, I'll wager, your most perfect mate.

DASHWOOD. If such a one draws breath, 'tis she. But this same Stickle keeps an eagle eye on her, repelling all advances which goes hard. Which brings me to the crux: I need your help.

LUSTFORTH. *(Aside.)* Aye, to an honest grave, thou poxy dog — "In face and form repellent — "? I'll repel thee from thy life!

DASHWOOD. Without some cunning pretext of propriety, I'll never get within her reach and all my hopes for love are lost. Sir Peter, what am I to do?

LUSTFORTH. *(Aside.)* But slit your throat and there's a start, y'canting cankered coxcomb!

LADY VANITY. *(Offstage.)* Husband! Coo-eee! Where hast thou gone, my stallion? *(At the sound of her voice, Lustforth freezes in his tracks. Pause. He gets an idea.)*

LUSTFORTH. *(Aside.)* Ha, ha! See now how I will use him for my sport. *(Aloud.)* Dick — You must live here with me.

DASHWOOD. Here, Sir Peter?

LUSTFORTH. Here. And I'll equip thee with thy newfound life and form thee as a tailor does the latest fashion. What say you to a music teacher? Yes, a genius of the arts. Henceforth wilt thou be known as Don Fidelio — A man of sterling reputation for whom love is as a foreign land: oft dreamt of, never visited. I'll put it out you are a distant cousin to my wife who has come hither for to master her in finer learning. *(Aside.)* And thereby master thee, thou knave!

DASHWOOD. Oh, 'tis an excellent device, good Lustforth. But your wife, will she not mind?

LUSTFORTH. Mind, my dear Fidelio? She hasn't got one! Wives have minds the like their husbands give them; mindful husbands give them none. But see your manner be not shy with her. She has a deep abhorrence of timidity. Fear not, as you instruct her, to make exorbitant demands. Be rough and ready in your nature, friend; be hard and it will please her well.

DASHWOOD. *(Aside.)* "Rough and ready"? "Make demands"? "Be hard and please her well"? What sort of husband's this?

LUSTFORTH. My home is yours, Fidelio! My comforts and my wife are here at your disposal. Use them as you would your house and dog.

DASHWOOD. *(Aside.)* I smell a rat. *(Aloud.)* You are too kind, Sir Peter.

LUSTFORTH. *(Aside.)* Aye, two kinds of face, the better to outface your plan.

DASHWOOD. *(Aside.)* Why does he mumble so and snicker 'hind his hand?

LUSTFORTH. *(Aside.)* I will be rid of you 'ere long, you cad, and tift the field.

DASHWOOD. *(Aside.)* I'll play along his game to see what fortunes yield. *(The two men smile at each other obsequiously and laugh.)*

LUSTFORTH. Fond Fidelio, come, let us go to her.

DASHWOOD. Loving Lustforth, lead the way. *(Exit.)*

Scene 2

The Lustforth home. Below stairs. Blunt seated in an arm-chair, blowing on a cup of tea and sipping. Molly Tawdry kneels before him, sucking his cock.

BLUNT. Say, Molly, you enjoy your work? *(Molly stops for a moment, then resumes.)* This geezer down the pub, heard him go on 'bout something he called Job Fulfillment. *(Pause.)* This doesn't usually happen to me.

MOLLY. Should I be doing something different? Tell me what you want.

BLUNT. *(Staring at him. Pause.)* D'you ever kiss?

MOLLY. I don't.

BLUNT. Na, it's important to have limits; otherwise, well, Christ knows what could happen. *(Pause.)* How many do you do a day? On average. Twenty? Thirty?

MOLLY. What's it matter, Mister Blunt? Counting 'em would mean remembering 'em and I don't like to. Only do as many as I need.

BLUNT. Yeah, why bother. Job satisfaction — useless as tits on a bull. And why stop there? Life satisfaction! You a happy human being? Name three people. I can't do it. Can you do it? Ask yourself enough times if you're happy, you'll be slitting your own throat.

MOLLY. All depends what keeps ya going I should think.

BLUNT. Oh? What keeps you going, Molly? Money? Food? A kindly look from strangers? Christmas crackers? Balmy breezes? The genius of Samuel Johnson? The color blue? The word "forever"? *(Molly stares at him in silence.)* What do I know of happiness? Life is an open sewer; only do my best not to fall in.

MOLLY. Should I be going then?

BLUNT. *(Producing a deck of cards.)* Here's one: Pick a card. Any card. Go on, Molly. I'll tell you what you got. *(Closing his eyes, conjuring.)* I see the color red — I see a number — No, a face. Hearts. I see a heart —

MOLLY. Wrong. Clubs. I don't like tricks.

BLUNT. Christ, I'm boring! Hell, I even bore meself. Was rather hoping — Technically, my mother bore me — Ever since she spat

15

me out into this world, I've yet to find one seemingly redeemingly worthwhileness to the long parade of tedium: My Life.

MOLLY. Why, what's so wrong with it?

BLUNT. See, once you get past all the staggering excitement of discovering when the sun comes up, there's light, and when it buggers off, its dark, there's really very little left worth writing home about. Assuming that you have a home. Assuming you know how to write. Assuming anyone gives two wet farts if you should live or die. 'Course there's love and marriage, kindness. But they're a hoax. Evil little carrot on a string to get me to sit up and give a toss what happens next on this green spinning ball of shite. I will say this, however — You have got one lovely arse. That's something worth the taking notice of. Of which one should take notice. Especially for a, what —

MOLLY. All right now. That's enough.

BLUNT. Was paying you a compliment.

MOLLY. I'll take my pay in cash.

BLUNT. *(Paying Molly.)* Ah, the grease that oils the cogs of life. What's the strangest one you ever had?

MOLLY. I'm looking at him, aren't I? Been coming here some months now and you never said a word. Cash on the table, get to work, and I don't mind. But here you are tonight —

BLUNT. I'm sick of the monotony!

MOLLY. Oh charming — I'll have to see a doctor now.

BLUNT. That isn't what I — Oh, I see. A joke.

MOLLY. I'm not the only one can be the object of derision.

BLUNT. You think I've been deriding you? Oh, Molly, no.

MOLLY. I'm no one's butt of ridicule. Think 'cos I'm dirt, I'm nothing?

BLUNT. Never nothing. God almighty. 'S'that the way I seem? What, condescending? Molly, underneath this shallow shell of mine I am completely empty. Barren. That's my title. Baron Void of Outer Desolation. There a point to my existence? Why the fuck am I alive? You say God's will, I'll clout you. What's He ever done? Give us arms so we can feel 'em empty, give us eyes to see we're all alone, give us hearts to have 'em shattered, give us life to fucking end it. God's a funny chap. No, Molly, you're much more than nothing. Wanted to see you in the hopes of — I don't know — jolting something. Oh, what's the point? Squirt my cum inside of you, I pay, you leave, I put the kettle on —

MOLLY. If I had known you wanted conversation, Blunt, I woulda

16

worn a hat. *(Blunt laughs.)*

BLUNT. Now that was good. That's lovely.

MOLLY. Why you look at me like that?

BLUNT. Wondering. What you'd look like. Without that silly dress.

MOLLY. Thought you were done. You want another go then?

BLUNT. No, I meant in regular — In boy's clothes.

MOLLY. Regular? You wear 'em.

BLUNT. But you are a boy.

MOLLY. Says who?

BLUNT. All right, have it your own way. Would you do it if I paid you? *(Pause. Off his look.)* So — You're happy in a dress.

MOLLY. Not be happy as a boy, I'll tell you that for nothing.

BLUNT. I'd like to see you happy.

MOLLY. *(Pause.)* I'll be going now.

BLUNT. No, don't —

MOLLY. Lay off the gin next time. *(Off his look.)* Can smell it on your breath. Blow on that cuppa all you like, I know what's in it.

BLUNT. Want some?

MOLLY. My mother lost her wits in Gin Houses. Carted 'er off and locked 'er up, they did. Least that's all Mistress Chissum told me. Never touch the stuff.

BLUNT. Mistress Jizzum?

MOLLY. Mistress Chissum's Corrective Home for Orphaned Children. Up in Huddersfield. Where I misspent my youth.

BLUNT. You ever considered any other line of work?

MOLLY. You're odd as two left feet. *(Pause.)* I used to have a fancy to be a lady's maid. Always reckoned them uniforms was swank. But that was — *(Blunt stares at her agape, then starts laughing.)* Right, that's it. You're off your bleedin' twig.

BLUNT. A lady's maid?

MOLLY. I'm off.

BLUNT. No, wait. A lady's maid you said?

MOLLY. T'ain't nothin' funny in it. Let me go.

BLUNT. Would you still do it if you could?

MOLLY. Said let me go. Yeah, would and all.

BLUNT. You would?

MOLLY. Who'd hire tat like me?

BLUNT. Herself needs a new maid. Could put in a good word.

MOLLY. What, her upstairs? Don't taunt me now. Don't bloody taunt me, Blunt.

BLUNT. I'm trying to help, you stupid bint. You don't believe me?

Here — *(Blunt rifles in a drawer and pulls out a pencil and paper. He calculates figures.)*

MOLLY. I reckoned you was shy the way you'd sit all quiet. Even when you spilled your spunk, never a moan or bloody whimper. Thought you was a mute. What's he got up in his head, I'd wonder. Now I'm like that sodding Noah in the raining fucking flood!

BLUNT. *(Holding out the paper.)* There! You see? That's what you could be making.

MOLLY. Did I ask you for your help? Did I say one — *(A bell rings. Molly starts.)* What's that?

BLUNT. It can't be six already. Christ. Herself will want her chocolate and the master his fried egg.

MOLLY. Off you go then.

BLUNT. She'll want to meet you.

MOLLY. Why you doing this? I can't.

BLUNT. You scared? What, nervous? Good. You should be. Means you want it.

MOLLY. Look, leave off. Go make her chocolate. They'll be angry if you're late. *(Silence. Blunt sits.)* What are you doing? They'll discharge you.

BLUNT. I don't care.

MOLLY. Yeah well I do. Don't need that on my conscience.

BLUNT. Moll, you know you want this job. The other bloke here knows it too.

MOLLY. *(Pause.)* I'd only fail.

BLUNT. 'S'that something new? I'm offering you a chance here. Take it. I'm not budging 'til you do. *(Pause. The bell rings.)*

MOLLY. All right! Enough. I'll do it.

BLUNT. *(Rising, excitedly.)* Don't you move. Won't be a tick.

MOLLY. Will — ?

BLUNT. Yes?

MOLLY. Why you doing this? What you want from me?

BLUNT. *(Smiling.)* You called me Will.

MOLLY. 'S'your name; so what? *(The bell rings again.)* Ne'mind. Go on.

BLUNT. I'll be right back. *(Blunt exits.)*

MOLLY. *(Looks around. Sits in the armchair.)* You stupid stupid slut.

18

Scene 3

The Lustforth home. Lady Vanity's closet. Lady Vanity at her vanity. Molly attending her. Blunt is happily humming to himself as he winds the many clocks in the room.

LADY VANITY. Prithee, Blunt, what time is it o'clock?

BLUNT. Gone two, your ladyship.

MOLLY. Madam, don't that make him now above an hour late?

LADY VANITY. Fie! The longer that he keeps from me, the deeper his regard. All they who would be good admirers know love's chiefest pleasure lies in its anticipation. But harkee, which of these two fans will show my eyes to best advantage — the Prussian or the French? Methinks the French for robin blue has always been a favored color to me; yet the darker hues of this, the Prussian, contrast well the paleness of my ample charms, like so —

BLUNT. *(Aside, to Molly.)* She means her tits.

LADY VANITY. And yet a woman should be somewhat mild methinks. A face is like a gun and one must exercise restraint where it is aimed, else it can break a heart without intention. I have broken scores with mine.

BLUNT. *(Aside, to Molly.)* And mirrors, too.

MOLLY. *(Aside, to Blunt.)* Stop it.

BLUNT. *(Aside, to Molly.)* It's not so much a gun as a cannon ball; it's packed with so much powder.

MOLLY. I say the Russian, madam.

LADY VANITY. Prussian, lass. A Russian wants no fan for 'tis an ugly people. I shall have beauty only to surround me; 'tis my element, you know. In beauty I have learned myself and proudly wear the aspect of my scholarship. The erudition of my form draws men to me like flitting moths to flame, but yet I spare their wings my fire's torment. For though devotion is their credit and one gains wrinkles saying, "no," a woman's charms, unlike her merits, must be enjoyed by one alone. And so I have, despite all protestation, sacrificed my life and my appearance to the singular dominion of my husband.

BLUNT. A mournful loss to all mankind.

LADY VANITY. But what think you of my new tutor, this

Fidelio? Is he not worthy, child? How like you his fine looks?

MOLLY. In truth, I've never seen so fine a gentleman. That face of his is handsome. His chest is wide and strong. His legs are thick with muscle and I'll warrant that between 'em —

BLUNT. *(Aside, to Molly.)* All right, Molly. That's enough.

MOLLY. To be perfectly honest, madam — When I first looked on him, I thought meself bewitched. If I was a fine lady, I'd be granting him whatever liberties he wanted, to be sure.

BLUNT. *(Aside, to Molly.)* But you're not a fine lady, so just see you don't.

LADY VANITY. Ah, but child, a man only pursues that which he cannot gain. No doubt you've witnessed how his eyes lewdly undress me; how they smolder with such anger at the thought of not possessing this my body with his touch. Betimes I am too kind when, sitting at my virginal for music lessons, I allow my hand to slip like so on top of his and he then feigns disgust to be polite. But 'tis a trick I know too well; my husband has employed it now for years. What time is it now, pray?

BLUNT. Two minutes more since last you asked.

LADY VANITY. Blunt, go to see if he is come. Methinks he must be in profoundest agony to keep away so long.

BLUNT. Yes, m'lady. *(Aside, to Molly.)* And you behave yourself. *(Blunt exits.)*

LADY VANITY. Ah, my life is a Greek tragedy. To be so blessed with such a face and have to watch men suffer. Prithee, fetch the ratafia, child. 'Ere dear Fidelio arrives to give my music lesson and profess his deepest love, I'll cool my body with hot spirits. Come fill, fill, fill, be not afraid; strong waters summon the Euterpean muse and charge my heart with lithesome measures.

MOLLY. I don't know what that means but it sure sounds lovely.

LADY VANITY. *(Toasting.)* To beauty in its every form. *(She drinks.)*

MOLLY. *(Aside.)* Ever since I first seen him, I can think of nothing else. Never happened to me before as most o'the types I've been with have been pigs. Grabbing, sweating, vomiting. But this refined young gentlemen — this Fidelio — Ladies, let me tell you —

BLUNT. *(Reentering.)* Don Fidelio, m'lady.

MOLLY. *(Aside.)* Later — Later —

LADY VANITY. Well, don't stand there like Mammon guarding treasure — Show him in! *(Dashwood enters, in the character of Don Fidelio, affecting an Italian accent. He bows.)* Sir, you surprise me at my levée! Is it one o'clock already? I have had no opportunity to beautify myself.

DASHWOOD. I've had no opportunity to wish to look at you, therefore fear not, signora. I come searching for a horse.

LADY VANITY. A horse? What, is my boudoir turned a stable?

DASHWOOD. Signora, that it could, for clearly you are making hay.

LADY VANITY. Ha ha — The wit of the Italian!

MOLLY. *(A coy little wave.)* Hey.

LADY VANITY. But we've our music lesson to assay. Signor, you cannot have forgot! *(Aside, to Molly.)* How quick he tries to hide the pained devotion of his heart!

DASHWOOD. Ah sí. How quick does pleasure slip one's mind.

MOLLY. *(Aside.)* How quick does pleasure fill my loins! *(Aloud.)* Sir, we are glad of your arrival. Be a shame to leave so soon.

DASHWOOD. *(Aside.)* What have we here? A juicy morsel to be sure!

BLUNT *(Aside.)* Why does he bat his eyes at him and blush like a young girl?

DASHWOOD. *(Aside.)* Nay, but I'd planned to ride to town to see Hermione today to woo her in this guise.

BLUNT. *(Aside.)* Look at him — Nervous, giddy, fumbling with his hands!

MOLLY. *(Aside.)* Ah, would I were the saddle on his horse so he could ride me well!

DASHWOOD. *(Aside.)* Hell's minions, what's the rush? She loved me then, she'll love me now, and still be there tomorrow. One small dalliance couldn't hurt. *(Aloud.)* Say, if my presence gives you pleasure, signorina, I would fein have opportunity to give you ample measure of it.

LADY VANITY. *(Aside.)* Faith, but I do apprehend his sly and subtle gambit! He's too shy to speak directly, so employs her as my proxy, wishing me to understand his passion without looking in my face. 'Tis clever — 'tis most clever! *(Aside, to Molly.)* Go on, girl. Give answer! *(Aloud.)* Signor, I'm willing that you should.

DASHWOOD. *(Aside.)* She's willing? What? Doth the lady pimp her maid? *(Aloud, to Molly.)* Speak for yourself, what say you, minx? Come, tell, you little jade.

MOLLY. Why, I would like that, sir, I'm sure.

BLUNT. *(Aside.)* My God, how can a common strumpet who has seen more cock than any army surgeon grow demure and coy like some dumb country bride? Don't tell me he's in love with him!

(Aside, to Molly.) You know, he takes you for a woman.

MOLLY. *(Aside, to Blunt.)* He can take me how he will!

BLUNT. *(Aside, to Molly.)* But then he'll find out that you're not one!

MOLLY. *(Aside, to Blunt.)* Not before I've had my fill! I may be young but yet I've got a trick or two stashed up my sleeve.

BLUNT *(Aside, to Molly.)* It's what you've got stashed elsewhere that'll be a rude surprise.

LADY VANITY. *(Aside.)* Oh, the ardor of his passion — I can scarce believe mine eyes! Now he kisses at her hand — those dulcet lips, that burning breath — I feel it on my body, ever craving more and more! Can I betray my husband? He will ruin me, I'm sure!

BLUNT. *(Aside, to Molly.)* Molly, please, don't do this.

MOLLY. *(Aside, to Blunt.)* I was hired for my service and so service him I must.

LADY VANITY. *(Aside.)* I'll melt — I'll swoon — I'll tumble — He'll reduce my heart to dust!

BLUNT. *(Aside, to Molly.)* But what about me? Molly?

LADY VANITY. *(Giggling demurely and fluttering her fan.)* Signor, cease these bold advances. You will compromise my name.

DASHWOOD. *(Aside.)* This lady's fairly addled! Yet I'll strive to win the game. *(Aloud.)* Fall to your music, madam. Put my teaching to the test.

LADY VANITY. *(Aside.)* He wants to hear me sing my love. *(Aloud.)* Signor, I'll do my best. *(As Lady Vanity sits at the harpsichord and prepares to play, Dashwood whispers to Molly and they go behind the screen.)*

DASHWOOD. I'll listen there behind that screen, not to distract my senses.

LADY VANITY. *(Aside.)* Poor man, he must avert his eyes to quell his lust's offenses.

BLUNT. *(After Molly.)* Molly, what are you doing? *(Aside.)* I cannot bear to watch this.

LADY VANITY. Are you ready for it now?

DASHWOOD. *(From behind the screen.)* Madam, I am standing at attention. If it be true that music is the food of love, spare not — But bang away, have at it, girl, and give me all you got! *(Lady Vanity begins to play and sing.)*

LADY VANITY. *(Singing.)*

How like a dove I'll sing,
And ease bring to your heart;
Then will I spread my wing,

And joined we shall depart.

BLUNT. *(Aside.)* This isn't happening! How can he do this? And after everything I've done. To pull him from the gutter, to get him a good job — What does he think I did it for?

DASHWOOD. *(Behind the screen.)* Oh yes — ! Like that! Like that!

LADY VANITY. *(Singing.)*
Tara-faldelalala, tara-faldelalala,
Our heart bound hand in glove;
Tara-faldelalala, tara-faldelalala,
Fore'er with you, my love.

DASHWOOD. *(Behind the screen.)* Bellissimo! The fingerwork! Right there!

BLUNT. *(Aside.)* Oh, I'll be sick! To think I cared and hoped that he — Oh Blunt you stupid fool! I'm burning up in hell and they're indulging in their fun! Well, if you poach my land, Dick Dashwood, I will poach yours in return. I'm no one's clown; I've had enough of playing his buffoon. From now on, if he wants to dance, it's Blunt who'll call the tune! *(Blunt exits.)*

Scene 4

Dame Stickle's home near Bishopsgate. Enter Dame Stickle and Lustforth.

LUSTFORTH. 'Tis eminently simple, dear Dame Stickle —

STICKLE. Nothing's ever simple, so be plain. You say a man will come — a man called Don Fidelio — ?

LUSTFORTH. He will attempt to flatter you to gain your niece's company.

STICKLE. By Jesu, now I see the machinations of this plot! But flattery's the devil's mischief — I will none of it. Why, just the other day the Reverend Puke preached a fine sermon on the evils of that vice. I am not the sort of woman men can flatter easily.

LUSTFORTH. I'faith, I doubt I could procure ten words of adulation for your person.

STICKLE. He would attempt my niece, would he? And during Lent at that? Ye gods — she is besieged by lechers like those Sabine

23

girls of yore!

LUSTFORTH. 'Tis why I've come to call on you: to offer you my help. I know you keep her guarded from the evils of this world.

STICKLE. I shield her as one fearless indefatigable fortress wall. But as the Bible tells, even the walls of Jericho can tumble to a force. We must be vigilant, dear Lustforth, and observe each tiny fault. If I've a crack in me, I beg you hunt to seek it out. And should you find my crack, good sir, I pray you fill it up.

LUSTFORTH. I fear the crack lies in your niece. In fact, of that I'm sure. And though 'tis certain to be slight, and guarded well and small and tight, I think it only fair and right to see that she is pure. Therefore, entrust her virtue to my care and I will fill her with devotion. Some pious friends of mine have planned a little celebration in observance of the holy day of Easter. With your permission I would like to have Hermione attend.

STICKLE. Ah, your canonical devotion does you credit, sir, indeed. Methinks she would not be so tempted if she spent more time upon her knees. But look you, here's your chance to probe her, sir, for forthward she doth come. *(Enter Hermione Goode, reading a letter.)*

LUSTFORTH. *(Aside.)* And forth doth lust engorge my loins!

STICKLE. Come hither, niece. What is the matter that you read?

HERMIONE. *(Quickly hiding the letter.)* No matter, Aunt Tiberia, but a letter from a doting childhood friend.

STICKLE. Say, if the letter doesn't matter, wherefore squirrel it away? Who is this friend? If 'tis Felicity Thrashbottom, see you, I'll be much displeased. The daughter of a fishmonger's too salty for your kind. By Jesu, girl, come give it me.

HERMIONE. Dear auntie, they're but silly words writ by a silly maid and no occasion for alarm.

STICKLE. Give me the letter, child. I'll be the judge of that.

HERMIONE. Judge not lest ye be judged for pride will come before a fall.

STICKLE. Dost speechify, Hermione? The devil can quote scripture.

HERMIONE. Dost thou take me for a devil, aunt?

STICKLE. Thou wear'st his frippery. Look you, Sir Peter, how she flaunts the features of her sex. By Jesu, talk to her. Instruct her to succumb.

HERMIONE. *(Aside.)* Oh how misfortunes follow me like dogs upon my heels. How can she wish me t'entertain so odious a man?

LUSTFORTH. Your dress, Miss Goode — I am against it.

HERMIONE. Sir Peter, so I see.

LUSTFORTH. I must be firm.

HERMIONE. You are, sir; therefore, do not press your point.

LUSTFORTH. She wants me to impel you to more modesty, my dear.

HERMIONE. Then you must say this letter has no cause to give her fear.

LUSTFORTH. And if I do, what will I get? Will you relieve my ache?

HERMIONE. Relief like that cannot be rushed. Have patience, for my sake. I promise to consider it. Now please, retract thy snake.

LUSTFORTH. Dame Stickle, your young niece's heart is innocent of guile. The letter's only shame, she says, lies in its grammar vile; she fears its crude deportment would offend your sense of style.

STICKLE. As you insist so I'll believe her, though Youth and Virtue rarely dine together at one table.

LUSTFORTH. Now good Dame Stickle, would you grant your niece and me some time alone? I would extend to her in quiet the invitation of which I spoke.

HERMIONE. *(Aside.)* By hell's own goblins, he means to take me to one of his Order's frightful orgies. The Knights of West Wycombe, or whatever the blast they're called. A bunch of sagging toothless men, debauching women in a cave and then proclaiming it a holy rite; I'd sooner join a convent and be manhandled by nuns! *(The bell rings.)*

STICKLE. By Jesu, who comes now and dares molest my door so loudly?

LUSTFORTH. Perchance 'tis that Fidelio of whom I gave you warning.

STICKLE. I'faith, 'tis he, for I've not heard my bell sound so depraved. Come quick, Sir Peter, you must help me drive him from my door.

LUSTFORTH. But dear Dame Stickle —

HERMIONE. *(Aside, to Lustforth.)* Go, Sir Peter. Go, and while you're gone, I will consider your firm offer.

LUSTFORTH. *(Aside.)* At last there's hope — And I have beaten Dashwood in the game!

HERMIONE. *(Aside.)* Consider it forgotten, sir, is what I mean. For shame! *(Lustforth kisses Hermione's hand and exits, followed by Dame Stickle.)* Now let me fall quickly to this letter and once more graze on its words. *(She retrieves the letter and reads.)* "Most virtuous Miss Goode — As birds do fly, as flowers bloom, as winter must give way to spring, so must my heart with gossip filled give voice to rumor on the wing." By my troth, a witty and a cryptic greeting! "The tittle-tattle of the town tells me you've been at mourning for the careless Captain Dashwood" — What, is my poor and broken heart but saucy food for chatter? "Fear not, blameless Hermione; whereas one person's scandal is another's treasure, if thou wouldst meet with me, I'd give thee an earful of pleasure!" Egad, though I don't understand, that sentence seems right naughty. "At three o'clock expect me at your garden gate and all will be revealed. Signed, X." Oh what a daring and a curious thing! And "X" — Whoever can it be? But now 'tis given three o'clock — Enough with speculation! Go find what at your garden gate may end your tribulation. *(Hermione exits. A cloaked figure enters up center, walking backwards, spying to see if anyone is about. Downstage, the figure turns and uncloaks. It is Blunt disguised as a fop in all his finery: wigged, powdered, in pink silk and satin ribbons.)*

BLUNT. *(Aside.)* Don't you fucking laugh! I know I look ridiculous, but this is what the rich fops wear. Those preening powdered pussy-boys who mince and prance and promulgate the fashion. Exchanging gossip, squandering family fortunes, and growling fear at anyone who tries to join their ranks like dogs in their proverbial mangers. *(With an affected foppish voice.)* "It is one thing, sir, to be a cattle merchant; quite another, though, to smell like one." *(An affected foppish laugh which turns into barking like a dog.)* Oh the nasty happy empty lives the moneyed classes lead. But now where is this precious Hermione Goode? She must have got my letter. I rang the bell and waited in the garden as I wrote I would, but — *(Hermione reenters. She sees Blunt and stops.)*

HERMIONE. *(Aside.)* Could this be him?

BLUNT. *(Aside.)* That must be her. *(Aloud, in his foppish voice; Bowing.)* Most gracious lady —

HERMIONE. *(Curtsying.)* Noble sir.

BLUNT. *(Aside.)* And now to teach that Dashwood a good lesson.

HERMIONE. Forgive me, sir, if I seem strange, but 'tis not every day I'm sent a letter of this kind. 'T'was unexpected and most curious; you use such bold pronouncements for a man I do not know.

BLUNT. Forgive *me*, lady, but you see I can't help being blunt. As to my name, dearest enchantress, 'tis — Horatio Pillowsoft.

HERMIONE. *(After a look aside.)* Oh yes, of course. I've heard of you. A pleasure, sir.

BLUNT. *(Aside.)* What's this? It seems the girl is better bred than

I had been expecting.

HERMIONE. You sometimes dine, am I correct, with lady — what's her name?

BLUNT. A lovely woman, isn't she? Of course she has her faults. She eats like a prized heifer.

HERMIONE. Does she really?

BLUNT. Oh my word! To see her with a bowl of custard can dispel your faith in God.

HERMIONE. And I believe that at the playhouse, sir, your box is next to —

BLUNT. — Just above him, actually. The theatre's divine!

HERMIONE. But come now, sweet Horatio, this rumor that you mentioned in your letter — ?

BLUNT. Oh I do love scandal, don't you, dear? Egad, yes, a most amusing tale concerning one acquaintance.

HERMIONE. I'faith, you have my interest piqued. Who is it, pray?

BLUNT. A charming chap! And such a jokester, to be sure. It seems a lady fell in love with him and he, as he is somewhat of a rake and likes love's liberties but not its ancillary duties, sought to throw her off by feigning his own death and changing his own name!

HERMIONE. He feigned his death and changed his name? All to avoid a lady? That is a jolly jest!

BLUNT. You see, she kept insisting he reform his ways and live with more sobriety, upbraiding him for wantonness —

HERMIONE. She sounds a perfect shrew.

BLUNT. But that is not the worst of it. For though she freely gave her heart, she gave him nothing else.

HERMIONE. Tosh, women these days set too much stock by their virginity and shame.

BLUNT. He used those very words himself! Though I attest that I myself could never treat a girl so harshly. His stories may amuse, yet I could never be like Dashwood.

HERMIONE. Never be — Whom did you say?

BLUNT. Captain Dick Dashwood, to be sure. But ah — I should have said Fidelio, for that's the name he's taken since he rendered Dashwood dead.

HERMIONE. Dick Dashwood is alive, you say?

BLUNT. Alive? Egad — to be sure. He's staying in the country with a boring oaf named Lustforth; a man who's soon to be a cuckold for he's thrown his wife at him. (Hermione weeps. Aside:) Now that wasn't supposed to happen.

HERMIONE. How could I have allowed myself to be such a damned fool?

BLUNT. Come, come, be not severe; all of God's creatures are damned fools. Why, I myself am scarcely better than a Bedlam donkey. Please don't cry like that. *(Aside.)* I hate myself right now. It's clear she really loves him and I, not thinking, barge in here with my dumb stupid plan —

HERMIONE. Oh, Horatio, I have been wronged. I thought in earnest he was dead. I grieved, I mourned, I wept. But now I see my heart has been kicked through the briarbush of care and stung with thorns of sorrow for a joke! Why is love, which should by all accounts bring happiness, such an unforgiving misery?

BLUNT. Here, have this handkerchief, Hermione, and dry your downcast eyes. That Dashwood's an unfeeling lout and don't deserve your sighs.

HERMIONE. You're only saying that because he is your friend. Men always vilify each other 'hind each other's backs. But when you're face to face, you'll laugh and call all women dupes. And that we are for loving you, in spite of your indignities.

BLUNT. I swear I'd never do such things. *(Aside.)* Oh, I have got some nerve when my whole character's a lie! I feel a hundred times more guilty than that Dashwood ever could! *(Aloud.)* I hate to see you suffer thus. By rights you should revenge.

HERMIONE. No, Pillowsoft; although 'tis sweet, revenge is not my game. Life is too short to waste it with delicious retribution. I'faith, 't'would be most pleasureful to teach him a good lesson.

BLUNT. I'faith, you should. 'Tis only fair. In fact, justice demands it.

HERMIONE. But how could I affect a heart so churlish, dead, and rancid?

BLUNT. I have a thought: Let's you and I assay this as a team. *(Stickle and Lustforth are heard offstage.)* — But what's that noise?

HERMIONE. Come quick, let's hide; you'll tell me of your scheme. *(Hermione and Blunt conceal themselves under Blunt's cloak as Lustforth reenters followed by Dame Stickle who is in a nervous dither.)*

LUSTFORTH. Dame Stickle, where has gone your niece? I fear the girl tries to avoid me.

STICKLE. *(A strangulated whisper.)* Sir Peter, did you see him?

LUSTFORTH. What? See who?

STICKLE. That man outside. A frightful stranger watching me from just beyond the garden gate.

LUSTFORTH. Who was he? Did you know him?

STICKLE. No, and yet he seemed familiar; and I don't like to be observed by people that I know. Tall and pale as death he was, and dressed all o'er in black; but no plain sensible black garment — It was laced and caped like Satan or some Irish Dancing Master.

LUSTFORTH *(Aside.)* Laced and caped in black? It cannot be! Pray heaven t'was not —

STICKLE. There, oh there — 'Tis he! No, no — Do not look back — ! *(Stickle has pulled Lustforth out of view. They peer around carefully and look.)*

LUSTFORTH. Dame Stickle, that's Fidelio! *(Hermione and Blunt peek out from behind the cloak.)*

STICKLE. The flatterer? Of course! You must protect me, Lustforth, from his hungry, carnal force. Ye gods and little fishes, when I think what he could do!

LUSTFORTH. We must go find Hermione and hide her from his view.

STICKLE. Those shifty eyes, that sinful guise — By Jesu, that ungodly bulge between his throbbing thighs! Oh Sir Peter, the vapors! Quick, my salts! To my room! *(Stickle and Lustforth exit. Hermione and Blunt reveal themselves.)*

HERMIONE. Egad, 'tis he!

BLUNT. Are you quite certain, dear Miss Goode, that you've the strength to face him?

HERMIONE. My knees do quiver, Pillowsoft — But yet I shall recover. Wish me good luck — *(Blunt kisses her hand.)* I come now to confront thee, Captain Dashwood, thou false lover! *(Hermione exits.)*

Scene 5

The garden of Dame Stickle's home. Dashwood, dressed as Don Fidelio, paces irritably.

DASHWOOD. O inconstant womanhood! O villainous deceitful spawn of Eve! I saw him enter in her house myself, that perriwig-pated peacock of a fop! I'll kill him. I'll kill them both!

But soft — ! *Io sono Don Fidelio;* so bury rage, hold to your task

— In spite of finding virtue dead and love a mask. *(Hermione enters, regards him briefly, then begins picking flowers. Dashwood rages.)* Well Madame, have you quite done with your pink prancing paramour?

HERMIONE. Who are you, sirrah, to thus trespass in my garden? 'Tis not a common country ramble or St. James's Park.

DASHWOOD. Lady, it is imperative I speak with you.

HERMIONE. Sir, I will not hear imperatives; it is a vulgar tense.

DASHWOOD. Come, come, Hermione, don't play coy games with me.

HERMIONE. Sir, I am not so poorly bred that any rantipole tatterdemalion can address me by my christian name. Be off with you. Or must I fetch a footman with a tumbril to remove thee from my lawn?

DASHWOOD. Deny it all you like, lady, but your deceit has been unmasked; and it is I, Dick Dashwood have discovered you at last.

HERMIONE. Sir, do not speak that awful name. I knew a man called Dashwood — All they who knew him swore that he would come to a bad end. 'Tis strange though now I look on you, you do possess some passing semblance to that wretched odious rat. But then, of course, you can't be he, for wicked Dick is dead.

DASHWOOD. Where do ye hide him, lady? Beneath your rosebushes perhaps, or crouching low behind your pansies? Marry, the air still stinks of his perfumes and noxious powders!

HERMIONE. Sir, you are clearly *non compos* and needful of a surgeon.

DASHWOOD. Aye, for then he can extract from me the heart which you have riven.

HERMIONE. A merry jest to cast a heart from one who never had one!

DASHWOOD. Whatever insufficiency lies in my heart, 'tis plainly of thy doing!

HERMIONE. What insufficiency is that? That thy heart lies? Thou wouldst not know the truth if thou were bastinadoed by it.

DASHWOOD. S'death, but thou art grown as cold and clever as a Stepney whore. I'll wager your new lover is to blame for that.

HERMIONE. As I know neither Stepney, sir, nor its attendant whores, I'll have to take your word on it! As to my cold and clever temperament — What would the man expect? He that did promise to reform himself, who swore he'd ne'er bring anguish or distress into my life and has, for all his lofty words, done very little else. What would that man expect after he'd bilked and cheated, lied and duped the one and only heart that could have found some good in him? Oh, how thoughtless and unnatural is man to have such expectation. And how foolish the dim poppet of a woman who would such a wretch oblige.

DASHWOOD. My dear Hermione, don't fault yourself for foolishness. But tell me that man's name and I'll forgive you all your wrongs.

HERMIONE. You? Forgive *me*? Pah! You listen, sir, as poorly as you love. You wish his name? Why, that is quickly done. His name is Don Fidelio.

DASHWOOD. Fid ... Madam, you tell a lie.

HERMIONE. Dost know the man? Come, come — If I do tell a lie, then prove it!

DASHWOOD. As you will. I'm Don Fidelio.

HERMIONE. Indeed. A moment past, you said you were Dick Dashwood.

DASHWOOD. True as well, for I am he.

HERMIONE. Dear monkey, listen well — A man may change his shirt and coat, even his wig, from day to day; I've heard of knaves and louts who change their lovers hourly. But changing one's own name shows a deceitful character.

DASHWOOD. And I tell thee, worse than a man assuming false identity is a dishonest little whore protesting at her chastity.

HERMIONE. Sir, you will keep a civil tongue or I will have you tried for slander.

DASHWOOD. Lady, I but wish you were my wife so I might beat the truth right out of you.

HERMIONE. If e'er I were so cursed, sir, I would hang myself instead.

DASHWOOD. Will you not change your mind, Hermione, and tell me that man's name?

HERMIONE. Unless you change your nature, sir, I've nothing more to say.

DASHWOOD. My nature, miss?

HERMIONE. Aye, cunning, guile, inconstancy! Only that Cerberus hath as many faces as thou hast. Which is the true? Look to it, sir! Look to it! Will you go?

DASHWOOD. In all good haste, dissembling witch. Farewell, Miss Goode.

HERMIONE. Farewell. *(They bow and curtsy to each other. Dashwood turns to go then stops and turns back.)*

DASHWOOD. What's that?

HERMIONE. You say?

DASHWOOD. What? I thought you said something.

HERMIONE. What, me? Just now?

DASHWOOD. Yes.

HERMIONE. No.

DASHWOOD. It must have been the wind.

HERMIONE. Yes, nature can be so —

DASHWOOD. Deceptive. *(They stand in silence.)* Well.

HERMIONE. Yes.

DASHWOOD. I hope he brings you all the pleasures, miss, that I myself could not. *(Dashwood storms off.)*

HERMIONE. A minute, sir! *(But he is gone. Surprise:)* Oh. *(Disappointed.)* Oh … *(Weeping, exiting.)* Oh!

Scene 6

The Lustforth home. Below stairs. A mess of dresses and plates of food. Molly is admiring his reflection in a silver tray. One of Lady Vanity's wigs is askew on his head. He sings.

MOLLY. *(Singing.)*
    — Then will I spread my wing,
    And joined we shall depart.
    Tara-faldelala, tara-faldelala —
(Molly indulges in a private fantasy. Blunt enters, dressed as Pillowsoft, and watches, unnoticed.) Why sir, how did *you* get in my room? A girl like me is not accustomed to such forwardness. What's that? Oh sir — Oh sir!

BLUNT. *(Stepping up.)* Well, I'll be buggered by the wrong end of a ragman's welly! Are we selling tickets to this spectacle?

MOLLY. *(Recovering from a start.)* And what are you got up as — A Christmas pudding?

BLUNT. That's incredibly unfunny and completely beside the point. What happened here?

MOLLY. What?

BLUNT. Happened! *(Lifting the dresses.)* As in this and this and this! Jumping Jehovah, I turn my back for one afternoon — What's

32

gotten into you?

MOLLY. Not what, Blunt. Who.

BLUNT. — Prancing around like the Queen of the May. I thought you'd given up whoring.

MOLLY. 'Course I've given up whoring! There's more to me than a good shag, you know.

BLUNT. It's him, isn't it? It's Fidelio. You're doing this for him.

MOLLY. What if I am? He knows beauty when he sees it and don't treat me like some cocking scrubber.

BLUNT. Oh my God. Are you really so daft as to believe that a posh set of manners and a kiss on the hand are the hallmarks of integrity? A powdered wig don't give a man good character and having wit don't give a man a heart.

MOLLY. Oh stop nattering on like a fart in a bottle. Pissing Jesus, one minute you're tossing m'life upside down, making me up as you like, and the next you're screaming blue murder 'cos I've done as you said. What do you want from me? You want me to leave then sodding well say so and I will!

BLUNT. I want you to stop turning my life into a complete and utter bollocks, that's what I want. All I have to do is think your name and I'm twitching like a spastic wond'ring where you've got to and what you've done. Every ticking moment of the day it's Molly Molly Molly without respite or a breath of calm. Try to keep my mind well-focused but soon as you walk in its hell and bloody chaos as my breath goes flat, my mouth dries up — It's like I'm —

MOLLY. You're in love with me.

BLUNT. In love with you? … Like hell!

MOLLY. You mope and mumble and give me these mean looks; you snap, you criticize, you look a mess and drink too much —

BLUNT. So what? And you don't like that?

MOLLY. I thought that we were friends.

BLUNT. I don't want friends! I want — *(Pause. Blunt suddenly grabs Molly and tries to kiss him.)*

MOLLY. Oi, I'm not a bloody loaf o'bread. You can't go grabbin' — *(Blunt releases him and steps away, ashamed. Molly stares at him.)*

BLUNT. *(Tenderly.)* Molly, I — *(Dashwood enters from the shadows, clapping his hands.)*

DASHWOOD. Bravo, signor — ! Bravissimo! If it isn't the Don Juan of Bishopsgate. Slumming, are we?

BLUNT. What do you want?

DASHWOOD. Your name, sir.

MOLLY. Don't you know'im? That's —

BLUNT. Horatio Pillowsoft, my lord.

MOLLY. Horatio what?

DASHWOOD. Well, Master Pillowsoft, deny it! Did you not this day at Dame Stickle's house corrupt one young Hermione, and through malign intent o'ersway the inclinations of her heart?

MOLLY. Hermione?

BLUNT. Corrupt? Look in a mirror, Captain.

DASHWOOD. Foh! — 'Tis fruitless to contest it for I followed you myself.

MOLLY. *(To Blunt.)* What you been doing?

BLUNT. He's demented.

MOLLY. "Master Pillowsoft"?

BLUNT. Look — No! I can explain this, Molly. Listen —

DASHWOOD. And what strikes me as most curious is that I should find you here. No doubt spreading more vile slanders for to blacken my good name.

BLUNT. Which name is that? It seems you take a new one every day!

MOLLY. You're one to point the finger, Master Pillowsoft!

DASHWOOD. Indeed, I will not stand to be dishonored thus. I will not conscience such ill-usage. *(Marching up to Blunt.)* Master Pillowsoft, my card — ! *(Dashwood hurls his card at Blunt's face in a challenge.)*

BLUNT. What, just the one? Here's fifty-two — *(Grabbing up a deck of playing cards, Blunt hurls them at Dashwood.)* — Now bugger off and all!

DASHWOOD. Sir, I demand satisfaction!

BLUNT. Satisfaction? You've had your bloody satisfaction, mate. Now the shoe's on t'other foot! How d'you like it? Bothered, are you? Serves you right, you puffed-up tosser!

MOLLY. *(To Dashwood.)* Don't mind him, sir. Ignore him. Come away and I can show you satisfaction.

DASHWOOD. Who are you, girl, and why are you pawing me with your grubby hands?

MOLLY. What?

BLUNT. *(To Dashwood.)* You watch your mouth, you!

DASHWOOD. I am speaking of a duel to remedy the calumny that you have heaped upon my name, sir, and the infamy you have brought to the stainless reputation of Miss Hermione Goode. Will you accept the challenge?

MOLLY. Don't you remember? It's me. Molly.

BLUNT. With all requisite pleasure, you fat oaf.

MOLLY. You and me behind the screen —

DASHWOOD. Shall we say pistols at dawn Wednesday week?

BLUNT. You can say porcupines up your bum for all I care.

MOLLY. You called me charming. Said I was your little minx —

DASHWOOD. Slut, will you desist?

MOLLY. But — What did you call me?

DASHWOOD. Farewell, sir. I shall look forward to blasting that annoying head from off its shoulders.

BLUNT. Oh talk to the fan. *(Dashwood exits.)*

MOLLY. *(Calling after him.)* But wait, don't you remember? How we — And you're not even bloody Italian, are you! *(But he is gone. Pause.)* I can't believe it. He called me a slut.

BLUNT. I'm a dead man, Molly.

MOLLY. Yeah, well, you had it coming.

BLUNT. You had *him* coming and he don't even remember you.

MOLLY. Oh, you're lower than a rat's bollocks, you are. For all the airs and graces, silks and satins you put on, you'll never be like him! You're vile, Blunt. You're nothing but a spiteful petty-minded servant and I wish I'd never listened to you or met you or laid eyes on you!

BLUNT. You're just saying that. *(Molly exits, weeping.)* Where are you going? Wait — what about this mess? You can't just — I did it all for you! *(Blunt removes his wig.)* Oh bugger bugger bugger! *(Aside.)* What are *you* looking at? Don't you know it's impolite to stare? Talk to each other, for God's sake. Take an intermission. I need to — House lights!

End of Act One

ACT TWO

Scene 1

The Lustforth home. Below stairs. Blunt is discovered, with his playing cards. An unopened bottle of gin before him. He reaches for the bottle and stops himself.

BLUNT. No. No, I mustn't. Mustn't mustn't mustn't. Pick a card, any card. I'll tell you what you got. The Queen of Misery, that's what. Who was the stupid pillock first thought love brings happiness? Love is scenes and screams and jealousy and acting like a cunt. I'll tell you a secret: No one has the first idea what makes 'em truly happy. "If only I was rich and tall and had a smaller bum." "If I had nicer clothes and whiter teeth and people laughed at all my jokes and wanted to have sex with me." If only if only if only. No. Seamus — That's the only bloke I ever knew was truly happy. Dear wee Seamus down the pub who, standing up, was all of four foot eight. Used to be a chimneysweep. Not much job fulfillment covered in soot, coughing up black phlegm and — to add insult to injury — one day he fell in love. Yeh. Down the lane and round the bend there lived the Widow Thwacker. Big as a bloody amazon, she was. Breasts like cannons and a face out of the Book of Revelations. Tortured him, she did. I tell you, it was nothing short of torture. And Seamus moping, pining, cursing his fate: Criminal. Finally, poor bleeder couldn't take it anymore. Got properly pissed as a Dutchman and, with a fist packed full o'daisies, he comes knocking at her door. She thinks he's havin' her on, so she cuffs him twice about the head and slams the door shut on his hand. Now, friends, a sensible bloke might, when faced with this, give up. But not our Seamus. No. Each Sunday for three months he comes and stands there at her door. And each Sunday for three months, she growls and hits him on the head. "Why do you mock me, chimneysweep?" she says to him at last. Know what he says? "I do not mock you, beauty. You are the goddess of my dreams, my every

36

waking hope's desire. You are truth made flesh and bliss incarnate. Widow Thwacker, I'm in love." I mean, for god's sake! And that's not the end of it, 'cos then and there he kisses her! On the lips! (Though considering his height, it may not have been the ones on her face.) And what did he feel at that moment? Pleasure? Arousal? Happiness? I'll tell you what he felt, he felt the marble bust of *Mister* Thwacker come crashing down on his head. And she brought it down with such enormous force that his wee brain became unstuck and rattled round inside his skull. Now he still sits at his same corner down the the local pub, but oh the grin he shines is one the like of which you've never seen. 'Course, he drools into his beer and wets himself when he forgets to go, but the Widow Thwacker's there beside him tending him with care, for (as she likes to say), "This Seamus is the happiest little bugger I have known." So I ask you, is that what a man must do to find his bliss? Is happiness only for children and the mentally deranged? Perhaps that is the price we pay to learn to be adults. What's an adult then but a sad and lonely git who doesn't have the merest clue of how to see or think or feel or talk to anyone at all. If happiness is born of innocence, I want it back. I want to run and laugh and dance and know that I'm alive. But more than that I want to know how to make Molly happy. I want to be the one who can. I want it to be me. So go on then: Pick a card. Any card. It won't make a sodding difference. Happiness — Hell, I'll drink to that. *(Blunt grabs up the bottle of gin, opens it and swigs.)*

Scene 2

Lady Vanity's closet. Lady Vanity at her harpsichord, completely drunk.

LADY VANITY. *(Singing.)*
    How like a dove I'll sing,
    And pum-pum la-di da —
(Calling.)
    Where art thou, mopus? Didst lose thyself in searching?
(Singing.)

Then will I spread my wing —
(Molly enters, carrying two bottles of brandy. He too is quite drunk.)
MOLLY. I wish you wouldn't sing that song. It's rubbish.
LADY VANITY. Thou art an angel sent from heaven, child. Come, fill the glasses high.
MOLLY. I was never one for drink afore, and yet this, rata-what-d'ye-call-it hath a bloody good effect. Puts me in mind of Christmas and me legs are all for dancing. Come, will ye jig with me, m'lady?
LADY VANITY. Molly dear, you must be potty. I've not danced these twenty years.
MOLLY. Have a drink then. There ye go. Come on now, missus — Up. Let's have ya. *(Molly guides Lady Vanity to her feet.)*
LADY VANITY. *(Laughing.)* — Oo my head's gone wobbles.
MOLLY. *(Leading her in a dance.)* Ready? And a one and a two and a —
LADY VANITY. Wait wait wait — What if my husband comes? Oh one can but hope.
MOLLY. You're wicked, you are. Not to worry, he isn't home.
LADY VANITY. He's never home these days — the bugger. Oop, mustn't use that sort of — Mummy said I'd get a spanking. *(Lady Vanity bends over. They giggle. Lady Vanity sits.)* Look at us: Two proper ladies in our prime brought low by drink and no one within earshot who could compromise our virtue. Harkee Molly, men are swine.
MOLLY. A curse on all their sex.
LADY VANITY. *(Hiccup.)* It wasn't ever thus, you know. There was a time, however *(Hiccup.)* brief. He wooed me. Sat for hours beneath the cherry blossoms and talked about — who knows. A woman never listens when she's *(Hiccup.)* falling in love. Oh what a curse is memory. *(Reaching a hand to Molly's face, almost kissing him.)* I swear, 'tis 's'if I'm looking in a glass. But you're not a glass now, are you; for I never was that young.
MOLLY. Ah go on — You've plenty life still in ye, madam. Why, your ladyship's the finest lady I have ever known.
LADY VANITY. Piffle! You, my child, have everything the whole world over longs for.
MOLLY. Me? *(Belches.)* Pardon. What have I got?
LADY VANITY. Your youth. The richest gift nature bestows.
MOLLY. For all my youth, I'll never have the amorous lovers that you do.
LADY VANITY. Amorous? Ha! Who pray?

MOLLY. Why, your music tutor. Fine Master Fidelio.

LADY VANITY. Filelio? Fiddle-faddle! I can't remember the last time a man looked at me with desire. Much as I fancy myself some great beauty, I don't fool a soul. Not even myself. *(Staring in the mirror.)* I've sat here with my perfumes, paints, and powders for so long, my face looks like a wedding cake that's been left out in the rain. Life is such a miracle; I've made a mockery of mine.

MOLLY. Bollocks … Your ladyship. Look — See those lips? Whose one smile lifts and lightens the air? See those eyes? Who else has such passion and care? *(Lustforth has entered unseen as Molly speaks.)*

LADY VANITY. Ask my husband. He'll give you her name.

LUSTFORTH. Aye, Molly, ask me.

LADY VANITY *(Sotto voce.)* Oh good God — Hide the bottles at once! *(Rising and going to him with open arms.)* Husband, dear!

LUSTFORTH. *(Pushing her aside.)* Out of my way, you drunk monstrosity. Egad, what sort of stews d'ye keep here, madam? Will ye swill me out o'house and home? *(To Molly.)* My girl, kindly inform this pulvilled ratbag who with impudence assumes the name of wife that I have countenanced enough!

LADY VANITY. See how he doth abuse me, Molly.

LUSTFORTH. Madam, you're drunk.

LADY VANITY. If I am drunk, sir, seek the cause within your self.

MOLLY. Your ladyship, I think I — I should go.

LUSTFORTH. No Molly, stay and list the fabulous delusions of this cow! What, does she weep, the monster? Lady, you'll need plaster with that water to patch up that crackled face.

LADY VANITY. Why do you speak me thus, my lord? Of what foul crime am I accused? That I have loved thee as a wife should love her husband all these years? I know you've taken mistresses. I've never said a word. And obviously the latest one has caused you now some grief. But is it good and proper, sir, to turn that grief on me? That is the action of a man, my lord, who'd kick a fawning dog.

LUSTFORTH. Make yourself easy, madam. I intend you shall have no more cause for such reproach.

LADY VANITY. That is my prayer, dear husband. You and I have lived too long to twist our hearts in mutual strife. Rather we should, like ripened vines, embrace each other to make peace and grow about the tree of age with comfort and with care.

LUSTFORTH. I mean to have our marriage vows annulled. *(Stunned, Lady Vanity slowly sits.)*

MOLLY. You cruel man.

LADY VANITY. No, Molly, please —

MOLLY. To speak to her with such disdain —

LADY VANITY. That is enough. Please go. *(Pause. Molly curtsies and exits.)* We are alone now, husband. Tell me, on what grounds seek you this action?

LUSTFORTH. Why i'faith, that I have given you the best part of my life and the repayment you have shown me isn't worth a pickled egg. *(Rummaging through her vanity.)* What is this? And this? And look at this! For all your potions, madam, you still smell like a damp grave. I tried to love you, lady, but look at you: like death, sitting in here with all your clocks, ticking away my life as though it's yours to waste. For years I hoped some sense of wifely duty would prevail wherein the bounty of an heir would be delivered to my house. Yet even in this simple obligation you have failed. Wherefore then have you any claim to call yourself my wife? A barren woman's like stale bread — only a blessing to the poor. So as I will not have my name and fortune die with me, I mean to have our vows annulled and wed more fruitfully. *(Lady Vanity rises and, with grace and dignity, makes to exit. She stops and turns.)*

LADY VANITY. My father warned me that you were a brutish man and that you sought my hand for the sole purpose of extinguishing your debts. For all the years he lived and breathed upon this earth, however, he could never have imagined you as capable of this. That you have taken, spent and ruined a considerable fortune which was left to me by him, I do not care. Those moneys were all mine to give and give them with my love I did, without condition or remorse. But e'er you wash your hands of me, Sir Peter, know this fact: Our marriage was not barren. I delivered you a child.

LUSTFORTH. Oh ho, perfidious bubble! You? Delivered me a child? That brandy must have crippled up your brain!

LADY VANITY. But two years after we were wed, I found myself expectant. The day I knew this to be true, my heart filled up with joy for thinking foolishly that I could win, by giving you an heir, a tiny portion of your heart. I sat out in the hall and waited breathlessly for your return. At seven the next morning, in you stumbled, drunk and loud. Her perfume was still on your clothes; her liprouge on your cheek. You looked at me and shouted, "Can't a man be left alone?" I came up to this room and vowed that so long as you could not love, I would not give a child to you to suffer heartbreak as I had. The next morning I informed you I had learned my aunt was ill and wanted me for company. Six months I stayed away, during which time I was delivered of a healthy beaming babe.

LUSTFORTH. This cannot be — That isn't true!

LADY VANITY. To live without my own dear flesh or your own love for all these years, I do not wonder that I drink. I am amazed I am alive. So do your worst — Annul our vows — Discard me as you will, and you shall never know your child, but die alone without an heir. For when a man's unloving, he doth make himself unloved. If that's thy fate: Despair. *(Lady Vanity exits.)*

Scene 3

The garden of Dame Stickle's home near Bishopsgate. Hermione enters with Stickle pursuing.

STICKLE. By sweet King Jesu, hussy, I will not let you refuse! Before your mother died, she made me swear to her an oath that I would raise you properly and see you decently disposed. And now you have a chance to make a suitable alliance —

HERMIONE. Suitable? Egad! Let's overlook for just one moment that he's almost thrice my age; let's overlook that he's a cretin; let's overlook that he smells bad; the fact he's got a wife already should repudiate his suit! And don't you mention that annulment — ! If a man may cast his wife aside whenever he should choose, what surety is left I will not meet an equal fate?

STICKLE. If more wives feared their husband's wrath, more marriages would last.

HERMIONE. A wrathful husband has one fate: to be made cuckold fast.

STICKLE.

    You churl! You slut! To wish him thus and question his intent?
    Has he not planned a sacred feast to mark the end of Lent?
    A celebration to unite as one all sinful errant souls,
    To save you from damnation and from hell's hot burning coals;
    And seeks he not your hand at that most sanctified of times — ?

HERMIONE. *(Aside.)* Oh here we go — I hate it when my aunt resorts to rhymes! She'll hear no reason, brook no logic, set her mind in stone —

STICKLE.

Attempt no disputation, girl. By Jesu, cease to groan!

God's providence has chosen you a husband in good time

To lift you from your sink of vice, your swamp of moral slime,

And with all pious pity place you properly beside

An ardent, wealthy christian man to be his blushing bride.

HERMIONE. Oh aunt, I beg you, cease this cadence. I can stand no more.

STICKLE. Then do as I instruct you, or I'll cast you from my door!

HERMIONE. He's old, he's fat, he's lecherous, he drinks, he uses snuff!

STICKLE. The choice is yours: Submit or you'll be destitute!

HERMIONE. Enough! *(Aside.)* Egad, this heptometrical prosody has rankled all my brain. *(Aloud.)* I'll do your will; I'll marry him.

STICKLE. Oh, my darling girl — Come, let me clasp thee to my breast. *(Aside.)* I wouldn't trust a word she says; this harlot's always lying. *(Aloud.)* On Easter day thou wilt be Lady Lustforth. I hope you shall conform yourself to all that will require.

HERMIONE. I will, for as in everything, obedience is king.

STICKLE *(Aside.)* Obedience my foot! But I will fadge some method to ensure the bond is set. *(Aloud.)* Be jocund, child. This alliance will provide you comfort and security. Your dead mother would be pleased. Now I must go discuss the banns with our good Reverend Puke. I'm sure he'll have a word or two of guidance for thine ear. I shall return forthwith, dear girl. Ah, praised be Jesu. Praise the king. *(Stickle exits.)*

HERMIONE.

Not only will she have me marry one my heart declines,

But she will also warp my mind in wedding metric lines!

What is happening to me? Must I, as woman, always sacrifice my will and serve? How could one wish me to wed Lustforth when it's clear that I love Dick? Perhaps you men think we poor women should be grateful for our lot. I beg you, ladies, educate these blinkered ignorants and show 'em that our dreaming souls run just as deep, our hearts beat equal measure. Not only equal, but much faster! Aye, you try wearing this tight corset for an hour to converse! And let's not overlook the shoes — Designed to keep us well off balance — that's man's pleasure, not our own!

Men want us tall and thin and pale with no breath for our voice.

What man in his right mind would ever dress like this by choice?

(Molly appears at the garden gate, disguised as a country maid.)

MOLLY. The young ward of this house, would you be she?

HERMIONE *(Aside.)* 'Od's Bodkins, now who comes to vex me? A country shepherdess who's lost her sheep? *(Aloud.)* Whom have I the honour of addressing, miss? *(Molly advances toward Hermione and circles her slowly, examining her closely.)* Was there something I could help you with?

MOLLY. Wot? No — I just came for a look. Yes, you're the one, I'd say.

HERMIONE. "The one"?

MOLLY. The pretty face, the stylish dress, the way you what's-it-called, comport yourself. That is a cracking hat, that is. How much that cost?

HERMIONE. *(Uncomfortable, opening her fan.)* I'm sure I wouldn't —

MOLLY. — Oo, a matching fan — Now that is swank! You look just like them portraits where they stand about with dogs.

HERMIONE. There must be some mistake, miss.

MOLLY. You're Miss Hermione Goode, i'n't'ya? The same Hermione Goode wot Master Fidelio's in love with — And Master Pillowsoft, as you like to call him, and God only knows who else. There — I can tell by the look in your eyes I'm exactly where I should be. Brought meself to see what such a prized young lady looks like.

HERMIONE. See here, who are you and how do you come to know all this?

MOLLY. *(With a touch of the dramatic.)* You may's well have't truth: My name is Molly Tawdry and I am The Other Woman.

HERMIONE. *(A slight pause.)* Other than what, my dear?

MOLLY. Other than you, for gawd's sake! Other than you in sharing Master Fidelio's embraces. Other than you in my devotion and my pain. He had his way with me, he did, and stole away my heart; then broke it like an old clay jug and will not know me since.

HERMIONE. Why do you come to tell me this? That the gentleman you speak of is a cad is hardly news. He wears a string of broken hearts upon his silken sleeve. And having sacrificed my own to that obscene and vile collection, I thought to nurse my wounds alone, but your words pour fresh salt in. Perhaps then you'll find pleasure in the fact that, 'gainst my wishes, I must soon take as a husband the most odious of men and face a future quite devoid of *any* passion, hope, or cheer.

MOLLY. Wot man? Who is it you must marry?

HERMIONE. Peter Lustforth! There, my dear. Now go rejoice at my misfortune.

MOLLY. Peter Lustforth? What, His Lordship? Why, he's old enough to be your father.

HERMIONE. So if it's sympathy you're after, you *have* come to the wrong house.

MOLLY. I didn't come for sympathy. I came and hoped that you'd be awful, ugly, crippled, greasy, fat — so that I could feel revenged in knowing I was right and he was wrong. But now I see you're strong and beautiful and, truth be told, I'm glad. I did not mean you harm, Miss Goode. All I wanted was to see the woman he's in love with. I wanted to see the woman I myself will never be. I'm sorry for your troubles, miss. Forgive me and good day. *(Molly turns to leave.)*

HERMIONE. No, please. Don't go. *(Hermione takes Molly's hand.)* There was more honesty in what you said than I have heard all year.

MOLLY. He don't deserve you, that Fidelio.

HERMIONE. That's very sweet, but we've just met and you don't really know me.

MOLLY. I know enough from what I've seen.

HERMIONE. You mean my matching hat and fan? Here, you can have them for yourself. But you mustn't judge a person by appearances.

MOLLY. Why not? The whole world does it all the time. I'n't that why gold is bright and shining and a pile of shit is not?

HERMIONE. Who are you, Molly? In your self. You must be someone of some strength to come to me like this.

MOLLY. What, me? I don't know as you'd like me much if you knew what I was. I i'n't like you, miss. I grew up in an orphan home. Never knew me mum and dad. One day I run away and landed on the streets. That's when I started selling.

HERMIONE. Selling what? Trinkets? Ribbons? Flowers?

MOLLY. Well, it was a kind of bloom.

HERMIONE. You can't mean —

MOLLY. I only had meself. After a while, it weren't so bad. 'Course, there's the hunger and the cold, and loneliness and danger, but I never knew much else. And being on the street, being nothing, no one looks at ya, 'cept for business. Too ashamed. And being like that, it gives you this strange freedom. Why, I could laugh or cry or pick me teeth and no one'd take no notice. But then this bloke, he tells me he could make something of me. Some proper work, some proper clothes, and here I am: a lady's maid. That's when I started feeling things that got me all confused. Now I can't walk just anywhere or sing or whistle. Now that the world looks different. Now that I've got my shame. It don't feel quite as free somehow. *(Pause. Molly reaches up and removes his wig.)*

HERMIONE. My God, but you're a boy!

MOLLY. Can I still keep the hat and fan?

HERMIONE. Did Dick know this when he and you — ?

MOLLY. Oh, no, miss, not at all! And promise you won't tell. Pretending to be a woman i'n't as easy as it looks.

HERMIONE. *(Laughing.)* You mean, he actually — Oh dear! Oh, that is marvelous indeed!

BLUNT. *(Off, as Pillowsoft.)* Miss Goode — ? Miss Goode, are you at home?

MOLLY. Shitstabbing Christ, I have to go!

HERMIONE. It's Pillowsoft!

MOLLY. He musn't find me here!

HERMIONE. Quick, don the hat and ope the fan and leave the rest to me. *(Hermione quickly helps Molly to put on the hat and open the fan, hiding his face, just as Blunt, dressed as Pillowsoft but messy and disheveled, appears in the doorway.)* Why, Master Pillowsoft! To what joy do I owe this sweet surprise?

BLUNT. Sweet as the bitter fruits of death, Miss Goode! Sweet as the anguish of an unloved heart! I come to bid a fond fare — Oh! I didn't know you had company. I offer my apologies. I bow. Again. Depart.

HERMIONE. This is my bosom girlhood friend up from the country for a visit. Allow me, sir, to introduce to you Felicity Thrashbottom.

BLUNT. *(Bowing.)* Felicitations, Miss Felicity; your humble servant, I. *(Molly giggles in falsetto and flutters his fan.)*

HERMIONE *(Pause.)* Don't mind her, sir. She's very shy.

BLUNT. A shy girl named Thrashbottom? And I thought I'd seen it all.

HERMIONE. You seem in a strange spirit, sir.

BLUNT. Strange spirits are in *me!* I hope that don't offend you, ladies. I did try to resist it. You see, Molly don't approve of drink, but —

HERMIONE. Molly?

BLUNT. He's — I mean, she's — Hell, bugger if it matters. I'll be dead soon anyway. This time tomorrow, in fact. With a bullet in my head. ('Least, I hope it's in my head because this suit cost me a fortune!)

HERMIONE. What do you mean, "a bullet," sir?

BLUNT. You haven't heard the news? Do you live under a rock? I have been challenged to a duel, Miss Goode, for having compromised your name. I could have just denied the fact, or given an objection. But then, he'd had his greasy way with someone that I cared for. So let us have the duel, says I, and I will fight you to the death! But then this morning as I woke, I felt a niggling worry. You see, I've never touched a gun, while he's a marksman, so I hear. So that's a tiny problem. No matter — Que será, será, as all those Spaniards say. I'd rather die for love than live unloved another day.

HERMIONE. But this is madness, dear Horatio. I beg you, sir, call off this duel. Apologize —

BLUNT. To him? I'd sooner eat my toenail clippings! All right, I'm sorry that I talk too much and tend to use profanity; I'm sorry I'm obsessed with sex and disrespectful to the rich; I'm sorry that I'm always late and too opinionated; I'm sorry that I'm lazy and I'm sorry that I'm scared. I'm sorry I'm short tempered, jealous, arrogant, and drunk. I'm also sorry I'm in love because I really wish I wasn't. For these things I'll apologize — To *you!* But not to him.

HERMIONE. But dear Horatio, if you should die, how would that profit Molly? Surely 'tis better that you should live and prove your love another way. Is that not so, Felicity? (*Molly shrugs and giggles in falsetto. Blunt stares at him blankly.*)

BLUNT. (*Pause. To Hermione:*) Is she a bit soft in the head? No — My only prayer, my dears, is to see Molly there tomorrow morning. For him to be the last thing on this earth I look upon. Then could I meet my maker with some dignity. Instead of shitting my pants with fear.

HERMIONE. Felicity, say something. I know your words could make a difference.

BLUNT. No dear ladies, I've imposed enough. Who knows, perhaps someday a perfect human being will be born who doesn't want and isn't scared of other people in his life. He'll be or have all that he needs, with hopes and fears and jokes and beds he doesn't wish to share. Thank God that isn't me, I say. And if he's born tomorrow, it's a good thing I'll be dead by then, 'cos if I lived, I'd kill him!

HERMIONE. Sweet Horatio —

BLUNT. No, no — I must get home to bed. If I don't get eight hours sleep, tomorrow I'll be dead. That was a joke. You're meant to — Fuck, I think I'm sober now. Adieu. (*Blunt exits. Hermione rushes after him.)*

HERMIONE. Wait, Master Pillowsoft — ! *(Turning on Molly.)*
How could you stand there and say nothing when he's suffering for
you? *(Rushing to the gate and calling.)* Master Pillowsoft, come back!

MOLLY. *(Lowering the fan and removing the hat.)* His name's not
Pillowsoft. It's Blunt. Will Blunt. Sir Peter Lustforth's valet. He's
the one wot turned me from a whore into a chambermaid.

HERMIONE. *(Pause; exploding.)* Is no one in this world whom
they pretend to be at all?

MOLLY. It seems I'm not the only one who judges by appearances.

HERMIONE. And how was I to know? He didn't act like someone's valet and he dressed —

MOLLY. — Like the pink fairy.

HERMIONE. People in glass houses, Molly.

MOLLY. We only ever pretend to be that which we truly are.
Appearances are everything. The rest is merely fact.

HERMIONE. Is he really Lustforth's valet? Well, I never!

MOLLY. Well, I have. That's how we met. Passed me corner seven
times before he had the courage to come up and —

HERMIONE. Spare me the gruesome details if you please.

MOLLY. T'weren't gruesome, miss. In fact, t'was rather sweet. Of
course I never trusted that. The nasty ones, the brutish ones, you
suss out right away. The nice ones, though — I never could be sure
exactly what he wanted.

HERMIONE. But now you do. He's only ever wanted you!

MOLLY. Yeh. The little bastard.

HERMIONE. You mean then you don't love him?

MOLLY. I didn't say that, did I now. I found his words affecting.
I mean, no one sees things in me like he does; like he knows me.
Like I'm beautiful. But then it seems that love and harlotry are not
so very different. In either case, they want to own you and posses
you for themselves.

HERMIONE. Are all men thus? Fie, let 'em find their deaths
then. We don't need men in our lives.

MOLLY. *(Making a joke.)* What's the alternative, miss — Me and
you? *(They stare at each other for an uncomfortable moment, then
each looks away.)*

HERMIONE. *(Hesitant.)* And why not? If they can do it, so can
we. I suppose that we could try. *(Pause. They sit beside each other.
An awkward silence.)*

MOLLY. I've never done a girl before.

HERMIONE. What, never? Nor have I. *(Silence. Finally and clumsily, they kiss. They consider it.)* We really don't need men at all.
MOLLY. I can't see why we bothered.
HERMIONE. They only bring us pain and strife.
MOLLY. We're better off without them.
HERMIONE. Though we'd be selfish not to help them.
MOLLY. Yeah — To save them from themselves.
HERMIONE. We owe it to our womanhood.
MOLLY. It shows that we're well-bred.
HERMIONE. If we don't do it, no one will.
MOLLY. Without us, they'd be lost.
HERMIONE. *(Pause.)* We'll need a plan.
MOLLY. Don't worry, pet. *(Tapping his head.)* I've got that sorted out.
HERMIONE. Then come, let's show the world of men what women are about. *(They rise to go, then stop and turn to the audience.)*
MOLLY *(Aside.)* Dear gentlemen, be grateful to your mistresses and wives —
HERMIONE *(Aside.)* Despite your vile behavior, it is they who'll save your lives. *(Exit Molly and Hermione, arm in arm.)*

Scene 4

A bleak and desolate heath at dawn. A single large bent tree. Fog drifts over the muddied ground. Distant ravens caw. Dashwood stands alone.

DASHWOOD. The cock hath crowed three times, yet he's not come. Is there no honour left? I have not wooed my bed this eerie night for fear it were my last; and now, as yon gray light breaks o'er the ghostly exhalation of the mist, it seems my perturbations were for naught. Yet she will marry Lustforth. Fie! Is there no end to shame? *(Blunt, dressed as Pillowsoft, wakes up behind the tree.)*
BLUNT. D'you mind keeping your soliloquy short, my friend? There's people trying to sleep.
DASHWOOD. Pillowsoft!
BLUNT. No, very hard tree root, actually. Gave me a crick in the neck.

DASHWOOD. I thought you weren't coming.

BLUNT. — As the nun said to the archbishop. No — I got here early and decided to try to sleep off this hangover. Didn't work. Some rectal leakage of a leather queen was waiting 'round to shoot me dead.

DASHWOOD. Sir, you have insulted me most grievously. Are you prepared to grant me satisfaction?

BLUNT *(Aside.)* She's like a bloody parrot, this one. *(A noise, off.)*

DASHWOOD. What ho — Someone approacheth!

BLUNT. I hope they're selling beer-eth. I could use a fucking drink. *(Singing.)* How like a frog I'll spring — *(Enter two footmen carrying a sedan chair, its window shaded. They set it down. Dashwood approaches it cautiously. The door of the sedan opens and Hermione emerges, hooded in a cloak.)*

DASHWOOD. Forgive me, lady, for the brashness of addressing you unbidden, but 'tis my duty as a gentleman to warn you against stopping in this dank and cursèd heath.

BLUNT. Yeh, there's a better heath just down the road.

HERMIONE. *(Unhooding her cloak.)* Gentlemen, repent!

DASHWOOD. Hermione — !

HERMIONE. I come not out of love for you, captain, but in the name of justice. I beg you gentlemen, forgive each other, lose this folly and let peace fill both your hearts.

BLUNT. Dick's always up for a piece, ain'tcha?

DASHWOOD. You waspish runt!

HERMIONE. Enough! Come, captain, take you this hand — *(He does.)* That's good. And Pillowsoft, the other. *(He does.)* Now through me as a conduit, let amity prevail.

DASHWOOD. Lady, I cannot let these insults go unchallenged. His wanton disrespect for me and for your reputation must be answered for, rebuked, and punished. Satisfaction is my right!

BLUNT. And yet you dress to the left.

HERMIONE. But sir, if I should take an oath no damage has been done; my virtue is unblemished; my reputation is still sound. Surely by rendering the reason void, the quarrel has no grounds.

DASHWOOD. The principle remains; I will not let it rest. And as you doubt the nature of my love, so let this challenge and its consequence obliterate mistrust and prove beyond all question that my heart is yours alone.

BLUNT. It's not your heart you have a problem keeping in your pants!

DASHWOOD. I'faith, thou blackguard, whoreson knave —

Come, let's not tarry!

HERMIONE. Dear sirs, since you will not be guided by compassion to assuage your lust for blood, grant me the role of Justice which, conferred, will function thus: to govern and administer this contest by sound rules, so the result of this dispute may be accounted right and true. What say you, gentlemen, to this?

DASHWOOD. I am agreed, Hermione.

HERMIONE. Master Pillowsoft?

BLUNT. *(Distracted.)* What? Oh. Yes. I really hoped Molly would be here for this.

HERMIONE. Then as this is my court of law, I call upon my bailiff! *(A dark shadow approaches from the mist. It is Molly, heavily disguised as an old dodderer: A wide brimmed hat, thick spectacles, a long robe, and a walking stick. He carries a leather case.)* Allow me, gentlemen, to introduce good Doctor Abel Quack who will officiate this trial by battle. Have you the pistols, doctor?

MOLLY. *(Affecting the voice of a doddering old man.)* Aye, that I do, young miss. Be these the parties to the quarrel?

DASHWOOD. We are, sir.

MOLLY. Which of these two gentlemen is he wot has been challenged?

BLUNT. That would be me.

MOLLY. As challenged, sir, you have the right to choose your ground.

BLUNT. I guess right here is good as any.

MOLLY. The challenger — *(To Dashwood.)* That be you, sir — may choose the distance from which both shall fire.

DASHWOOD. I choose ten paces.

MOLLY. Right. *(Molly goes to Blunt to begin measuring ten paces. Blunt regards him curiously.)*

BLUNT. You look familiar, doctor. Do I know you?

MOLLY. Ever had the clap, my son?

BLUNT. No, sir.

MOLLY. I doubt it then, as that be my stock in trade. Why the number of diseased cocks, penises, pikes, knobs, rogers, todgers, pillocks, pokers, wimbles and brat-getters I have seen. I can recognize a geezer by his quimstake at ten paces, sir, and —

HERMIONE. Doctor, if you please — ?

MOLLY. Right. Ten paces it be. *(Molly draws a line with his walking stick. Dashwood takes his ground.)* I shall prepare the pistols now. *(Molly steps aside with the leather case to load the pistols. He passes by*

Hermione. To Hermione, sotto voce:) How'm I doing?

HERMIONE. *(Sotto voce, to Molly.)* A little less local color, I think. *(Aloud.)* Dear sirs, as one or both of you may not survive this duel, this is your opportunity to make your peace with God. If you have ought to say, then I beseech you, speak it now.

DASHWOOD. What I do here, Hermione, I do but for your love. I pray the memory of me will live on in your heart as that of one who loved you in despite of all your faults. The only words left on my lips hold all the sadness of my shattered heart: Farewell to all that might have been.

BLUNT. *(Pause.)* Well, I certainly can't top that. I'd just like to say —

MOLLY. *(Stepping forward with the case.)* The pistols be ready, gentlemen.

HERMIONE. No, no, doctor. Do let him finish.

BLUNT. I have no great poetry in me. I only ever read two books in my life. And one of them was a book of matches. I've never traveled or seen the world, though I have seen heaven once or twice in the company of … of a certain someone. So if that's where I'm going to, I'm not afraid of it. It's the most beautiful place I can think of. *(Pause.)* Thank you.

MOLLY. *(Opening the case; to Blunt.)* Choose your weapon, sir. *(Blunt takes a pistol. Molly goes to Dashwood and presents him with his pistol.)* Miss Goode — *(Hermione produces a handkerchief.)* Upon the dropping of this handkerchief from Miss Goode's hand, you may commence to fire. Gentlemen, cock your pistols and take aim. *(Dashwood cocks his pistol and takes aim. As Blunt awkwardly struggles to do the same:)*

BLUNT. I can't believe it. My last moments on this earth and he don't care enough to be here. That stupid sodding —

MOLLY. Miss Goode, at your discretion. *(Hermione holds out the handkerchief. The following is a rapid whispered aside:)*

BLUNT.
Oh what a mess I have made of my

BLUNT and DASHWOOD.

Life

DASHWOOD.
Is o'erturned from all pleasure to

DASHWOOD and BLUNT.

Strife

BLUNT.
Surfeits all of my sense.

51

DASHWOOD.
    Will this be fair recompense?
MOLLY and HERMIONE
    These fools must be schooled
    and a bit ridiculed
    for the way that they're ruled
    by their
MOLLY, HERMIONE and DASHWOOD.
                    Passion
DASHWOOD.
                        Compels me to seek
DASHWOOD and BLUNT.
                                Satisfaction
BLUNT.
    He wants. Will my death be that
BLUNT and DASHWOOD.
                        Action
DASHWOOD.
    Is all that is left.
HERMIONE. *(To Molly.)*
    Remember now, nuance
MOLLY. *(To Hermione.)*
                    and deft.
HERMIONE and MOLLY.
    We will teach them what happens when they tell a lie.
DASHWOOD and BLUNT.
    Oh dear God, please don't tell me I'm going to die!
(Hermione drops the handkerchief. Blunt and Dashwood fire.
Hermione cries out. Dashwood is felled. Molly rushes to feel his pulse.)
BLUNT. Oh my God! Is he dead? I'm sorry — I'm so sorry — Tell
me he's not dead!
MOLLY. As a doornail, my son.
BLUNT. What have I done — Oh Christ, what have I done —
HERMIONE. *(Rushing to Blunt.)* Quick, you must leave at once
or face arrest by the authorities.
BLUNT. But —
HERMIONE. Don't you understand? The name of Pillowsoft will
now forever be that of a hunted man. It is murder you have done
here — Go!
BLUNT. *(Not sure whether to run or stay.)* Murder? But — Look,
are you sure there's nothing that can be — Oh shit oh shit oh shit!

(Blunt exits, running. Hermione rushes to Molly's side, over Dashwood.)

HERMIONE. How is he, Moll?

MOLLY. He should be waking up in just a minute. He'll be a bit confused, but he's all right. You should go now, miss.

HERMIONE. You're certain he's not badly hurt?

MOLLY. Not from a plug of tow. It only knocked him out a bit. Good thing I saw to it his pistol would misfire.

HERMIONE. Poor Blunt seemed scared out of his wits.

MOLLY. Let's hope enough to rid him of that Pillowsoft for good. *(Dashwood moans and stirs.)* He's waking now.

HERMIONE. You're certain you can manage all the rest of this alone?

MOLLY. You coached me well, Miss Goode. Don't worry. I know what to do.

HERMIONE. *(Leaning down and stroking Dashwood's face.)* For what comes next, you have my pity. But I do it all for you. *(Hermione rushes to her sedan chair and exits.)*

MOLLY. *(Tapping Dashwood on the cheeks.)* Captain Dashwood, can you hear me?

DASHWOOD. *(Waking.)* Who are you? What happened? Am I dead?

MOLLY. You fainted, you silly faggot. You been out an hour but are unharmed.

DASHWOOD. Egad! And Pillowsoft?

MOLLY. Your bullet blew his head clear off. Exploded like a melon. No, do not rise quite yet. I have some troubling news. As I scrutinized your body to make sure you were not hit, I discovered a condition.

DASHWOOD. A condition? What is it?

MOLLY. Alas, you have the pox, dear captain. Known also as the French Disease. One gets it from lewd intercourse. It be my expertise.

DASHWOOD. What? The pox, you say? But that's impossible!

MOLLY. I be sorry it be true. And there's not much I can do, for to be honest, well — You're through.

DASHWOOD. But Miss Hermione — And her impending marriage to Sir Peter at the sacred meeting of the Order of the Knights of West-Wycombe — ! The pox? Oh, why could not that bullet have destroyed my life instead? Now I must watch as that old toad and my dear love are wed! *(He weeps.)*

MOLLY. Come, sir, I'll walk you home. That's right, you let it all out. Have a good cry then. Old Quackie's here. *(Aside.)* There's folk for whom life's plenty, and they never ask for more; but then there's him, who's got it all, and is really quite a bore! *(They exit with Dashwood weeping on Molly's shoulder.)*

Scene 5

At the mouth of the caves of West Wycombe. Lustforth appears dressed as the Roman God Mars — in armor, wearing an enormous false phallus and carrying an ornate horned helmet. He addresses his brother knights.

LUSTFORTH. Oh Ostara, Ostara! Most holy Order of the Knights of West Wycombe! By the grace of Angerona and Harpocrates, Gods of Rome and Egypt of stern silence, I welcome thee, ye brother knights, who gather to pay homage to our Saxon sister Eostre who this day in the body of a hare lays forth her fertile eggs of blesséd spring. Brothers, rejoice! For I, in form of Mars, that son of Juno, God of war, do this day claim in conquest my beloved bride of Venus. Oh brother knights I charge thee, solemnize this marriage day with all forms of carnality, and plow forth every virgin hole to make Priapus proud! *(Putting on his helmet and raising his arms.)* In Venus' loins, by Hell's annointed — *(The answer is given by the brother knights: "Keep we our spirits true!")* To the caves, brothers — To the caves! Let the orgy commence! *(Lustforth produces a curved horn and blows it loud. The interior of the cave is revealed: Large statues of Pan and Priapus with enormous full erections, a fountain of Venus streaming water from her vagina, sconced torches in the form of breasts, several tunnels extend further into the cave, their entrances carved into the shape of the parted legs of women. The overall motif clearly a celebration of sex and fertility. Dashwood enters dressed as Apollo.)* Apollo, you look apoplectic. Have you come hither for to mourn your loss or see my conquest eternized?
DASHWOOD. I, sir, unlike some of my brother knights, would ne'er betray the honour of another of our membership. I come to celebrate Ostara.
LUSTFORTH. Oh how Dame Fortune doth bestow her smile on

my exalted line, for I'll soon have Hermione abed and breeding sons. The Lustforths will be ever great!

DASHWOOD. Indeed, sir; for you are the greatest fools, the greatest liars, and the greatest beasts in the whole world and I heartily desire that you were out of it!

LUSTFORTH. Ah Dick, thou poor Aesopian fox to curse the grapes thou canst not reach. Enjoy the orgy — If thou canst! — whilst I go find Hermione who's guised as lovely Venus. I joy tonight to know I'll soon impale her on my penis! *(Lustforth exits into the tunnels from which the sounds of music and an orgy in progress can be heard. Dashwood sits, his head in his hands. Molly and Hermione enter on the other side of the stage. Molly is dressed as Doctor Quack and Hermione in Molly's chambermaid outfit, carrying a mask which, as they speak, Molly helps her tie in place.)*

MOLLY. I shouldn't worry. She'll be here. I helped her dress the part myself.

HERMIONE. Yes but she's late! Are you certain that she'll come?

MOLLY. She wants her husband back, though bugger me if I know why.

HERMIONE. *(Seeing Dashwood.)* Oh by God and all the saints — 'Tis he! How shall I — What shall I say? No, Molly, I'm not ready!

MOLLY. Cease your fussing, miss. You know the plan.

HERMIONE. It'll never work. How do I look?

MOLLY. Just like a chambermaid, miss: Utterly forgettable. Now go! *(Molly gives Hermione a shove toward Dashwood.)*

HERMIONE. *(Pause. Attempting a common accent.)* Excuse me, sir. I doesn't mean to interrupt you sitting there.

DASHWOOD. What's that? Oh not at all. It's Molly, isn't it? *(They smile at each other awkwardly and look away. Molly makes talking gestures to her, urging her to speak.)*

HERMIONE. You broke my heart, you know. *(Molly smacks his hand to his face in resignation.)* Girl like me's ought to have better sense. But then I'm nothing but a chambermaid, sir, and we believes all wot we sees. We gives our hearts and that's our ruin.

DASHWOOD. No, Molly. The blame is mine. It is the curse of my own nature.

HERMIONE. Your nature, sir?

DASHWOOD. Who are you, honestly? Who am I? We wear these masks and mad disguises, striving to be true. But which face is the true and which the false? How could I, in seeking to give pleasure, cause so much distress?

HERMIONE.   P'raps because of who you've sought to give that pleasure to.

DASHWOOD.   You mean myself. Then I am no more than a hopeless cad.

HERMIONE.   No one's truly beyond hope, sir.

DASHWOOD.   Ah Molly, there you're wrong. For she whom I adore is to be married on this night and my own death is drawing near.

HERMIONE.   Yeh. The pox. *(Off his look.)* Everybody knows. *(Lady Vanity enters from the back, dressed as Venus. She sees Hermione and, thinking she is Molly, tries to get her attention, as Molly tries to get her attention.)*

LADY VANITY.   *(In a loud whisper.)* Hsst — Molly!

HERMIONE.   *(Diverting Dashwood's attention.)* But come, sir — P'raps a brisk walk under the night sky might relieve your melancholy.

DASHWOOD.   Very well, dear Molly. Lead the way. *(Just as Hermione and Dashwood turn to exit, Molly yanks Lady Vanity behind the statue with her and covers her mouth. Hermione and Dashwood exit.)*

LADY VANITY.   *(Pulling free of Molly.)* Unhand me, you ruffian! I will have you whipped!

MOLLY.   Your ladyship — You're late!

LADY VANITY.   Molly? Oh thank heavens. I've had the tortures of the damned getting here tonight. The house is in an uproar.

MOLLY.   Why? What's happened?

LADY VANITY.   *(Noticing a statue.)* Oh now that is tacky. What? It's Blunt: He's gone. Quit his post. And without notice. Muttered something about finding Sir Peter to demand his pay and then disappeared, leaving my toilet in an absolutely ghastly state.

MOLLY.   Gone? But he can't have gone — Where would he — Your ladyship —

LUSTFORTH.   *(Appearing in the tunnel.)* Sir, take your hands off there. The lady is spoken for. *(Molly bows low and exits quickly as Lustforth approaches Lady Vanity. He kisses his way up her arm. She opens her fan and scuttles away downstage.)* Come now my gentle Venus, be not modest in thy ways. Soon shall we two be man and wife and joined together as one flesh. Wouldst thou be churlish, sweetest child, and disallow a tiny taste?

LADY VANITY.   My lord, we women must reserve ourselves; for like the grocer with his choicest goods, we must guard well against a fickle touch.

LUSTFORTH. No fickle touch drives my love's hand. You've but to put me to the test to find my love is rigid, dear Hermione.

LADY VANITY. But call me "wife" and not that name and I'll endeavor so to do.

LUSTFORTH. I'll call thee wife and nymph and goddess. I'll do anything you say.

LADY VANITY. Will you agree upon a contract?

LUSTFORTH. Speak the terms and I'll obey. *(Aside.)* Egad, but she's so supple, firm, so ripe, and so alive! I'faith, her very scent renews my heart and makes me young. *(She produces a contract.)*

LADY VANITY. Impremis, sir, to be my husband and to claim me as thy bride, all thy devotions and attentions must exist on me alone.

LUSTFORTH. My darling, I would have it be no other way, in truth. And as a testament to my true ardor, let me seal it with a kiss —

LADY VANITY. My lord, your breath is sour; please stand off. Next item: lovers.

LUSTFORTH. Lovers?

LADY VANITY. Lovers. I'm still quite young, sir, and I'll need to have diversions. A woman must be ever free to wander, stray, or roam; a husband is fair company, but best when left at home.

LUSTFORTH. But dearest heart, cannot my love provide you all the passion that you need?

LADY VANITY. Of course it can't, my darling! What odd pleasure could I ever hope to gain from such a sagging sack of tired flesh? You have my hand, the rest is mine to give to whom I choose. You'd do the same if you were young and standing in my shoes. *(With that, Lady Vanity gives him a quick kiss on the cheek and exits into the tunnels leaving a shell-shocked Lustforth.)*

LUSTFORTH. "Sagging sack of tired flesh" — ? But — but my angel! My darling! Wait! *(Lustforth chases after her as Dame Stickle enters cloaked, opposite.)*

STICKLE. By Jesu, 'tis a curious place to hold a marriage service! I hope the Reverend Puke hath found his way and is not lost. O'er craggy rock and through a tangled wood I had to step and 'tis so dark in here my eyes must take a moment to adjust; yet I will see to it the hussy's wed if 'tis the last thing that I do! Hark, is that music that I hear? Doth someone play upon an organ? Egad, by good John Bunyan, could the service have begun? It seems to come from over there. I'll just creep over quietly and squeeze in at the back. *(Stickle exits into one of the tunnels. From offstage, the sounds of the orgy: men panting, women giggling and moaning. Pause. Stickle emerges from the cave in a state of shock.)* Holy Christing Mother of God! There's twenty, thirty of them there and not a one with shame! Bodies heaving, bodies writhing, twined in every carnal shape — with legs and breasts and mouths and buttocks and some quite enormous — *(She sees one of the statues and lets out a scream. Turns. Another statue. Another scream.)* Oh by sweet Jesu, I'm surrounded like poor Daniel in the den! What sights are these of lechery, what hellish lustful din! Oh save me Jesu, save me from this pit of flesh and sin! *(Stickle exits into the tunnel as Lustforth chases a laughing Lady Vanity across the stage. Blunt enters dressed as himself, followed by Molly, still as Doctor Quack.)*

BLUNT. *(Calling.)* Sir Peter!

MOLLY. And I am telling you, Master Pillowsoft, it isn't wise for you to be here, sir. Dost know there is a warrant and a bounty for your capture?

BLUNT. The name's not Pillowsoft, it's Blunt. I am a valet, not a gentleman; a servant, not a fop. And Sir Peter owes me money, doctor. Soon as he settles his account with me, I'm buggering off. Yes, I know there is a warrant out. And let them take me if they will.

MOLLY. But what about this — this Molly person that you spoke of? Won't she care?

BLUNT. Why should he? Never has before. Besides, he'd never speak to me, now that I've shot the man he loves. *(Calling down one of the tunnels.)* Sir Peter!

MOLLY. You'd never have shot him if you'd minded your own business! How can you be so sure this Molly was in love with him?

BLUNT. You never saw his eyes atwinkle at the mention of the name Fidelio. The way he'd blush and laugh. That's love. No sir, you don't know Molly like I do. *(Calling down another tunnel.)* Sir Peter! Where the devil can he be?

MOLLY. By gum, you moan on and on about love so much, it's a wonder you have any time left to feel it.

BLUNT. Forgive me Doctor, I must go.

MOLLY. Running away won't solve a thing! You can't run from your heart.

BLUNT. And what's to keep me, Doctor, eh? Look about you! The rich all run in golden circles, chasing their gilt tails; the poor swim in the dark, hoping the waters aren't too septic. Man has a soul, yet lives as hollowly as a conch which only holds the echo of the sea. My heart? I'll drink it away. Or go in there and lose myself in hedonistic pleasure. With any luck I'll end up dead from drowning in a pool of spunk.

MOLLY. Gibbering Jesus, Mister Blunt, when I think of all the genuine misery in this world! You have your health, a decent job, what more d'ye want? Happiness? Then sodding well be happy — No one stopping you but your bloody self. Moping around like a misery-guts, drinking gin out of bloody teacups as if you're fooling anyone —

BLUNT. But what chance do I stand? I mean, hell, look at me! I'm certainly no prize.

MOLLY. Know thyself and love thyself and others then just might.

BLUNT. Wait a minute. How'd you know about the teacups? You've talked to Molly, haven't you? You've seen him!

MOLLY. *(A pause of panic.)* Go away!

BLUNT. You have! Where is he? Come now, Doctor, have you no mercy in your heart? I'll be forever in your debt.

MOLLY. *(Turning to go.)* You are quite the most annoying man that I have ever met!

HERMIONE. *(Entering, leading Dashwood.)* We must have taken a wrong turn, sir. Perhaps this way —

BLUNT. … Molly?

LUSTFORTH. *(Offstage.)* Hermione! Dearest! Whither dost thou fly? *(Molly and Hermione [leading Dashwood] run off in opposite directions. Blunt follows Hermione. Lustforth enters, searching and out of breath. Aside:)*

　　They say a younger wife can make you young again. Behold:
　　We're not yet wed and this Hermione has made me twice as old!
(Lady Vanity, still dressed as Venus, appears.)

LADY VANITY. Your bride awaits under the stars; will you not take her, mighty Mars? *(Lady Vanity exits. Lustforth pursues as Stickle enters. Seeing each other, they scream. Lustforth exits.)*

STICKLE. By all the sinful turpitude of Sodom and Gomorrah! Why, every bend reveals another sweaty fornication — With moans and cries and lips and thighs and fingers probing places I don't dare to verbalize! I must to find the Reverend Puke so he might save their errant souls! *(Turns to go. Stops.)* But what if the Reverend can't be found? Can I abandon these sad sinners to the pleasures of their holes? What would King Jesu do if faced with all that flesh? Why, surely he would lead them from temptation to remorse. I must go back to save them. 'Tis the only righteous course. *(Exiting.)* I come in the name of the lamb, my children. Satan, get thee behind me! *(Blunt has entered, lost and searching, as*

the sounds of the orgy in the cave grow around him.)
BLUNT. … Molly? Where did you go? Where are you? Molly? Molly — ?

Scene 6

Outside the mouth of the cave, at the foot of a large budding tree. Just before dawn. Hermione is still disguised. Dashwood sits sadly at the foot of the tree.

HERMIONE. Look how the wet and newborn day doth struggle on unsteady legs. Say, can these infant beams of dawn not spark some measure of rekindled hope within your heart?

DASHWOOD. My thoughts are fixed as stagnant waters, Molly. Your words remind me too much of my loss.

HERMIONE. Happiness is but a choice. To love is to be of this world and learn its mysteries.

DASHWOOD. Ah, but life is not so simple. There are far too many questions.

HERMIONE. All you have to do is ask them. Close your eyes and ask one now.

DASHWOOD. Fie, close my eyes?

HERMIONE. Or are you scared? Come, prove that you are brave enough to open up your heart. Here, use this scarf. I'll help you with it. Kneel — *(Dashwood kneels as Hermione blindfolds him with the scarf.)*

DASHWOOD. I feel a fool. *(Pause.)* A proper question. From my heart. *(Pause.)* Am I, in spite of all my conquests and the women I have known, to die alone, unloved at last? Is there no hope for me to find, in some small measure, absolution for my wrongs? Oh this is hell, this vanity! What care I for forgiveness when I traded care and comfort for a momentary thrill? I merit no one's love. In my soul there's but one hope: That kind and fair Hermione has found true happiness at last. For she who knows me best received it least, deserves it most. If I could have a surety of that, a sign —

HERMIONE. A kiss? *(Having removed her mask, Hermione kisses him gently. Dashwood pulls off the blindfold and regards her in surprise.)*

If thou canst find it in thy heart to grant forgiveness to thyself, I will forgive thee too. Then shalt thou know that I am truly happy.

DASHWOOD. If this be a dream —

HERMIONE. Then take this hand and let us dream together always. We've both suffered quite enough.

DASHWOOD. But what about the —

HERMIONE. Sshh. You do not have the pox, dear captain. You may take my word on it. *(They kiss. Blunt enters from the cave with a length of rope fashioned into a noose. He tries to hook the other end onto a branch of the tree.)* Mister Blunt, what are you doing?

BLUNT. Me? Nothing. I was — Did you say Blunt? Miss Hermione, you know my name?

DASHWOOD. It seems there's little that she doesn't know.

BLUNT. And Captain Dashwood! But you're —

DASHWOOD. Very much in love.

BLUNT. I shot you and you fell! They told me you were dead!

DASHWOOD. *(Stepping forward, his hand extended.)* Sir, I offer you the hand of peace.

HERMIONE. What are you doing with that noose?

BLUNT *(Warily shaking Dashwood's hand.)* Oh you mustn't bother yourself, miss. Only I was in there looking for a stalactite from which to hang myself. Problem is, I don't know which are stalagmites and which the stalactites. I know one goes this way and one goes that, but —

LUSTFORTH. *(Off.)* Enough! Enough! I can run no further! *(Hermione quickly masks herself again with Dashwood's help as Lady Vanity, dressed as Venus, exits the cave followed by Lustforth.)*

LADY VANITY. But mighty Mars, you said you would do anything to have me as your bride —

LUSTFORTH. Wouldst have me chase thee to my grave?

LADY VANITY. Tut tut, Sir Peter — All because I voiced a couple trifling conditions —

LUSTFORTH. Trifling? Egad you galloping shrew, even the treaty of the Austrian Succession had not as many codicils as those which you set forth! Oh what ill spirit was it did infect mine eye and make me think you meek? How could I leave my wife for you? At least the woman could stand still! I used to say she was a monster for I treated her as such. For all I've done, I should be punished, but I will not marry you. I'd rather face the rack and have that torture end my life. But you'll not be my torturer — For that I want my wife!

LADY VANITY. Methinks we'll have the marriage now.

LUSTFORTH. Egad demonic wench, but are you deaf? Out of my way!

HERMIONE. Quick Blunt, bring me that rope! *(As Lustforth makes a dash for it, Dashwood and Hermione grab him as Blunt runs about him and ties him up.)*

LUSTFORTH. What, Blunt, you're here as well? What in the name of Judas are you — Help! Help! Murder! Help!

MOLLY. *(Rushing on, still dressed as Doctor Quack.)* Will? Will? Is someone hurt?

LUSTFORTH. *I'm* hurt! I'm ambushed! I'm betrayed! I'm — *(Blunt stuffs a handkerchief into Lustforth's mouth, silencing him.)*

BLUNT. He's fine.

HERMIONE. Good doctor, are you not as well a doctor of divinity?

MOLLY. Divinity, affinity, cupidity, duplicity — I am a doctor of all things. You wish me to officiate a marriage?

LADY VANITY. Make that two.

LUSTFORTH. *(Gagged.)* Mmm-mmm, mm-mm!

MOLLY. The bridegroom seems most eager. Would both the couples stand together arm in arm to pledge their troth. *(Lady Vanity takes Lustforth as Dashwood and Hermione join hands.)* Ah what a lovely sight it is. So much better than a clapped out dong. Do both you ladies take these men to be your lawful husbands, to love and cherish before heaven and in every way be true?

HERMIONE and LADY VANITY. We do.

MOLLY. And do you gentlemen take these fair ladies as your lawful wives, to love and cherish before heaven and in every way be true? *(Lady Vanity ungags Lustforth.)*

LUSTFORTH. A plague on both your spouses! I won't be made to wed, sir! You can't force me, I am already married!

LADY VANITY. But Sir Peter, the annulment —

LUSTFORTH. I'll annul the annulment! Hell and blast, look at me, girl. For all my bragging bluster, I can't satisfy your youth. My knees are weak, my back is sore, my teeth are falling out. To bring thee pleasure might just kill me. Go and find someone who can. For who would want this sad old carcass when there's so much more to life?

LADY VANITY. *(Removing her disguise.)* I do, Sir Peter. I do. For no one knows you like your wife. *(Pause.)* See how he stares agape without a word to say! You poor sad fool — *(She kisses him.)* Now put the gag back in; I liked him best that way.

BLUNT. *(Gagging Lustforth.)* Now that everybody's sorted and has everything they want — And everybody's happy; that is, everyone but — *(A lascivious laugh off stage. Dame Stickle exits the cave, her clothes half off, holding a dildo.)*

STICKLE *(Entering; laughing.)* Poor Reverend Puke, it seems you've reached your limit and I'll have to finish off myself. *(Stickle spits on the dildo and is about to insert it when she turns and sees the assembled company.)* Oh bugger.

HERMIONE. Aunt Tiberia?

LADY VANITY. Good heavens, it can't be!

HERMIONE. What are you doing here? What's happened to your clothes?

STICKLE. I — that is to say — well — by Jesu, they fell off! I was all alone in the dark trying to feel my way around when a gentleman bumped into me. Actually, four of them did. Several times. I think I pulled a muscle, but — Dear God, is that Fidelio? My girl, what has he done to you?

HERMIONE. Auntie, this is Captain Dick Dashwood. The man I love and am going to marry.

STICKLE. Are you mad? Love has no place in a marriage, my girl. *(To Dashwood.)* Get away from her. Shoo! Shoo!

LADY VANITY. Mistress Chissum, is that you?

STICKLE. Oh my Christ! I know that voice. Mrs. Breakwater?

LADY VANITY. *(Grand.)* Chissum — Where is that baby?

MOLLY. Mistress Chissum?

HERMIONE. What in all creation — ? Lady Vanity, this is my aunt, Dame —

LADY VANITY. Chissum, almost twenty years ago I came to you in Huddersfield and, posing as a Mrs. Breakwater, left a baby in your charge. Every year I sent you moneys for that child's upkeep and care. I also wrote you letters, but you never answered one! And so I ask you, Chissum, where the devil is my son?

STICKLE. Mrs. Breakwater — Lady Vanity — Children are such trouble and ungrateful little wretches. I did all that I could, but then one day, they ran away and I've not seen them since. Then when my sister died, God bless her, and I was saddled with my niece, I took the name of Stickle and interred my past with peace. But I beg your pardon, lady, and I don't mean to correct you, but the baby that you brought was not your son. It was your daughter.

LADY VANITY. You think I wouldn't recollect the sex of my own child?

STICKLE. It has been almost twenty years and maybe you forgot.

LADY VANITY. What rot and rubbish — It was a boy!

STICKLE. I'm sorry, no. It was a girl.

BLUNT *(Aside.)* My money says it was a handbag.

HERMIONE. Ladies please! Restrain yourselves. Whether a boy or a girl —

MOLLY. It was a boy indeed — *(Molly removes his disguise. He is dressed beautifully — and as a boy.)* — And his name was Valentine.

LADY VANITY. My son!

MOLLY. *(Running to her arms.)* My mother!

BLUNT. My Molly!

STICKLE and DASHWOOD. My God.

LADY VANITY. Did I not say that looking at you was like looking in a glass? Oh yes, hold me, dear child, hold me if you pardon all that's past.

BLUNT *(Aside.)* In classical terms, this is what's called a Homo ex Machina.

LADY VANITY. Sir Peter, may I present to you your son and rightful heir. Lord Valentine, say hello to your father. *(Molly removes the gag from Lustforth's mouth.)*

LUSTFORTH. Oh my darling boy. My heart swells up with pride to look on you, and yet I hang my head in shame. Can you ever forgive an old selfish fool for all the hardships you have faced? I would embrace you, son, but as I'm rather tied up at the moment —

MOLLY. May I untie him, mother?

LADY VANITY.

Untie him; free his heart, my son. Unite us all as one.

Though keep the rope for later, Peter, and we will have some fun.
(As Lustforth is untied, Blunt steps forward to the audience.)

BLUNT. *(Aside.)*

Kind ladies and dear gentlemen, our little play is done.

I hope we've brought you pleasure, or at least offended none —

MOLLY. *(Going to Blunt.)* What d'you think you're doing, Will?

BLUNT. The epilogue. What does it look like!

MOLLY. Well stop it. We're not finished yet.

BLUNT. Dashwood has Hermione, the Lustforths have each other and in you, they found their son, and Chissum-Stickle over there has found the joy of sex. What more is there to do?

MOLLY. I swear you flap your gums so much, it's a wonder your mouth don't fly off your face! *(Pause.)* Me and you.

BLUNT. Oh we don't have to do that scene.

MOLLY. Yes we do, Will. Learning to be a woman has made a better man of me. A man who can recognize beauty and isn't afraid of goodness. A man whose heart is open and willing to take a chance.

BLUNT. I always reckoned you could take care of yourself.

MOLLY. But then who'd take care of you, you daft cow? *(Pause.)* Marry me, Will.

STICKLE. What? You can't do that! He's a man. It's a sin!

LUSTFORTH. Even worse — He's a servant, my son! The disgrace!

HERMIONE. Can't you see they're in love?

DASHWOOD. Yes, be still.

LADY VANITY. Show some grace.

MOLLY. *(Suddenly producing a hand of cards.)* Pick a card, Will. Any card. If I get it right, you'll marry me.

BLUNT. *(Pause.)* Happiness is a choice. I choose — *(Blunt picks a card. Looks at it. Pause.)*

MOLLY. The King of Hearts.

BLUNT. *(Pause.)* You. *(Blunt takes Molly in his arms and they kiss.)*

End of Act Two

Epilogue

MOLLY.
Kind ladies and dear gentlemen, our little play is done.
And while I know it's getting late and you all want to run,
I'd like to beg another tiny moment of your time
And bear with me and this, our evening's last atrocious rhyme.
Oh never mind — Look, go be happy. Love is everywhere.
I know that sounds cliché and dull, but really I don't care.
The world is full of pain and fear, but you could make it grand
By simply opening your eyes, your heart, your soul, your hand
And telling someone that you care and that we're here together.
For life is short and love is sweet. Give pleasure without measure.

End of Play

PROPERTY LIST

Feather duster
Play program
Tray
Bottle of wine
Cup of tea
Deck of cards
Pencil and paper
Clocks to wind
Wine glass
A letter
Flowers to pick
Wigs of the period, male and female, to lay about
Dresses of the period, to say about
Calling card
2 bottles of brandy
Bottle of gin
Various objects on vanity table
Lady's fan
Lady's hate of the period
Sedan chair
Walking stick
Leather case
Pistols for a duel
Handkerchief to hold pistols
Curved horn to blow
Mask
A contract
Length of rope fashioned into a noose
Man's handkerchief
A dildo

SOUND EFFECTS

Bell ringing
The caw of ravens in the distance
Organ music
Sounds of an orgy (moaning, groaning, etc.)

NEW PLAYS

★ **MATCH by Stephen Belber.** Mike and Lisa Davis interview a dancer and choreographer about his life, but it is soon evident that their agenda will either ruin or inspire them—and definitely change their lives forever. "Prolific laughs and ear-to-ear smiles." –*NY Magazine.* "Uproariously funny, deeply moving, enthralling theater. Stephen Belber's MATCH has great beauty and tenderness, and abounds in wit." –*NY Daily News.* "Three and a half out of four stars." –*USA Today.* "A theatrical steeplechase that leads straight from outrageous bitchery to unadorned, heartfelt emotion." –*Wall Street Journal.* [2M, 1W] ISBN: 0-8222-2020-2

★ **HANK WILLIAMS: LOST HIGHWAY by Randal Myler and Mark Harelik.** The story of the beloved and volatile country-music legend Hank Williams, featuring twenty-five of his most unforgettable songs. "[LOST HIGHWAY has] the exhilarating feeling of Williams on stage in a particular place on a particular night...serves up classic country with the edges raw and the energy hot...By the end of the play, you've traveled on a profound emotional journey: LOST HIGHWAY transports its audience and communicates the inspiring message of the beauty and richness of Williams' songs...forceful, clear-eyed, moving, impressive." –*Rolling Stone.* "...honors a very particular musical talent with care and energy... smart, sweet, poignant." –*NY Times.* [7M, 3W] ISBN: 0-8222-1985-9

★ **THE STORY by Tracey Scott Wilson.** An ambitious black newspaper reporter goes against her editor to investigate a murder and finds the *best* story...but at what cost? "A singular new voice...deeply emotional, deeply intellectual, and deeply musical..." –*The New Yorker.* "...a conscientious and absorbing new drama..." –*NY Times.* "...a riveting, tough-minded drama about race, reporting and the truth..." –*A.P.* "... a stylish, attention-holding script that ends on a chilling note that will leave viewers with much to talk about." –*Curtain Up.* [2M, 7W (doubling, flexible casting)] ISBN: 0-8222-1998-0

★ **OUR LADY OF 121st STREET by Stephen Adly Guirgis.** The body of Sister Rose, beloved Harlem nun, has been stolen, reuniting a group of life-challenged childhood friends who square off as they wait for her return. "A scorching and dark new comedy... Mr. Guirgis has one of the finest imaginations for dialogue to come along in years." –*NY Times.* "Stephen Guirgis may be the best playwright in America under forty." –*NY Magazine.* [8M, 4W] ISBN: 0-8222-1965-4

★ **HOLLYWOOD ARMS by Carrie Hamilton and Carol Burnett.** The coming-of-age story of a dreamer who manages to escape her bleak life and follow her romantic ambitions to stardom. Based on Carol Burnett's bestselling autobiography, *One More Time.* "...pure theatre and pure entertainment..." –*Talkin' Broadway.* "...a warm, fuzzy evening of theatre." –*BrodwayBeat.com.* "...chuckles and smiles of recognition or surprise flow naturally...a remarkable slice of life." –*TheatreScene.net.* [5M, 5W, 1 girl] ISBN: 0-8222-1959-X

★ **INVENTING VAN GOGH by Steven Dietz.** A haunting and hallucinatory drama about the making of art, the obsession to create and the fine line that separates truth from myth. "Like a van Gogh painting, Dietz's story is a gorgeous example of excess—one that remakes reality with broad, well-chosen brush strokes. At evening's end, we're left with the author's resounding opinions on art and artifice, and provoked by his constant query into which is greater: van Gogh's art or his violent myth." –*Phoenix New Times.* "Dietz's writing is never simple. It is always brilliant. Shaded, compressed, direct, lucid—he frames his subject with a remarkable understanding of painting as a physical experience." –*Tucson Citizen.* [4M, 1W] ISBN: 0-8222-1954-9

DRAMATISTS PLAY SERVICE, INC.
440 Park Avenue South, New York, NY 10016 212-683-8960 Fax 212-213-1539
postmaster@dramatists.com www.dramatists.com

NEW PLAYS

★ **INTIMATE APPAREL by Lynn Nottage.** The moving and lyrical story of a turn-of-the-century black seamstress whose gifted hands and sewing machine are the tools she uses to fashion her dreams from the whole cloth of her life's experiences. "…Nottage's play has a delicacy and eloquence that seem absolutely right for the time she is depicting…" –*NY Daily News.* "…thoughtful, affecting…The play offers poignant commentary on an era when the cut and color of one's dress—and of course, skin—determined whom one could and could not marry, sleep with, even talk to in public." –*Variety.* [2M, 4W] ISBN: 0-8222-2009-1

★ **BROOKLYN BOY by Donald Margulies.** A witty and insightful look at what happens to a writer when his novel hits the bestseller list. "The characters are beautifully drawn, the dialogue sparkles…" –*nytheatre.com.* "Few playwrights have the mastery to smartly investigate so much through a laugh-out-loud comedy that combines the vintage subject matter of successful writer-returning-to-ethnic-roots with the familiar mid-life crisis." –*Show Business Weekly.* [4M, 3W] ISBN: 0-8222-2074-1

★ **CROWNS by Regina Taylor.** Hats become a springboard for an exploration of black history and identity in this celebratory musical play. "Taylor pulls off a Hat Trick: She scores thrice, turning CROWNS into an artful amalgamation of oral history, fashion show, and musical theater…" –*TheatreMania.com.* "…wholly theatrical…Ms. Taylor has created a show that seems to arise out of spontaneous combustion, as if a bevy of department-store customers simultaneously decided to stage a revival meeting in the changing room." –*NY Times.* [1M, 6W (2 musicians)] ISBN: 0-8222-1963-8

★ **EXITS AND ENTRANCES by Athol Fugard.** The story of a relationship between a young playwright on the threshold of his career and an aging actor who has reached the end of his. "[Fugard] can say more with a single line than most playwrights convey in an entire script…Paraphrasing the title, it's safe to say this drama, making its memorable entrance into our consciousness, is unlikely to exit as long as a theater exists for exceptional work." –*Variety.* "A thought-provoking, elegant and engrossing new play…" –*Hollywood Reporter.* [2M] ISBN: 0-8222-2041-5

★ **BUG by Tracy Letts.** A thriller featuring a pair of star-crossed lovers in an Oklahoma City motel facing a bug invasion, paranoia, conspiracy theories and twisted psychological motives. "…obscenely exciting…top-flight craftsmanship. Buckle up and brace yourself…" –*NY Times.* "…[a] thoroughly outrageous and thoroughly entertaining play…the possibility of enemies, real and imagined, to squash has never been more theatrical." –*A.P.* [3M, 2W] ISBN: 0-8222-2016-4

★ **THOM PAIN (BASED ON NOTHING) by Will Eno.** An ordinary man muses on childhood, yearning, disappointment and loss, as he draws the audience into his last-ditch plea for empathy and enlightenment. "It's one of those treasured nights in the theater—treasured nights anywhere, for that matter—that can leave you both breathless with exhilaration and…in a puddle of tears." –*NY Times.* "Eno's words…are familiar, but proffered in a way that is constantly contradictory to our expectations. Beckett is certainly among his literary ancestors." –*nytheatre.com.* [1M] ISBN: 0-8222-2076-8

★ **THE LONG CHRISTMAS RIDE HOME by Paula Vogel.** Past, present and future collide on a snowy Christmas Eve for a troubled family of five. "…[a] lovely and hauntingly original family drama…a work that breathes so much life into the theater." –*Time Out.* "…[a] delicate visual feast…" –*NY Times.* "…brutal and lovely…the overall effect is magical." –*NY Newsday.* [3M, 3W] ISBN: 0-8222-2003-2

DRAMATISTS PLAY SERVICE, INC.
440 Park Avenue South, New York, NY 10016 212-683-8960 Fax 212-213-1539
postmaster@dramatists.com www.dramatists.com